THE
MANCHESTER GUARDIAN
A CENTURY OF HISTORY

CHARLES PRESTWICH SCOTT.

Editor of the *Manchester Guardian* since 1872.

From a photograph taken in 1920.

THE
MANCHESTER GUARDIAN

A CENTURY OF HISTORY

BY

WILLIAM HASLAM MILLS

With a Special Introduction for the American Edition

BY

CHARLES PRESTWICH SCOTT
Editor of " The Manchester Guardian" since 1872

GREENWOOD PRESS, PUBLISHERS
WESTPORT, CONNECTICUT

The Library of Congress has catalogued this publication as follows:

Library of Congress Cataloging in Publication Data

Mills, William Haslam.
  The Manchester Guardian.

    Appeared first in the Centenary number of The
Guardian, May 5, 1921.
    1. The Guardian, Manchester, Eng.
PN5129.M33G85 1972   072.7'2   74-137067
ISBN 0-8371-5530-4

PN5129
M33
G85
1972

Originally published in 1922
by Henry Holt and Company, New York

First Greenwood Reprinting 1972

Library of Congress Catalogue Card Number 74-137067

ISBN 0-8371-5530-4

Printed in the United States of America

To

CHARLES PRESTWICH SCOTT

To bring the dispositions that are lovely in private life into the service and conduct of the commonwealth ; so to be patriots as not to forget we are gentlemen.

EDMUND BURKE
in *The Present Discontents.*

—for the growing good of the world is partly dependent on unhistoric acts ; and that things are not so ill with you and me as they might have been, is half owing to the number who lived faithfully a hidden life and rest in unvisited tombs.

GEORGE ELIOT:
The concluding words of *Middlemarch.*

The author is indebted to the proprietors of the " MANCHESTER GUARDIAN " for permission to republish this brief history which appeared in their Centenary Number on May 5, 1921.

Contents

Illustrations

INTRODUCTION TO THE AMERICAN EDITION

I AM perhaps the last person who should write a prefatory word to this admirable book of my friend and colleague, Mr. Haslam Mills. In it he has written much which is not only of great interest as a picture of the social and political development of the country for a hundred years reflected in the life of a newspaper, but he has displayed all this, inevitably no doubt, from that newspaper's standpoint and with myself as in some sort its director for half of the period.

But in spite of this all too personal interest in the work and its subject I cannot deny myself the pleasure of adding a few words for the American Edition. It seems such a friendly thing to have an American Edition and that it should be taken for granted that quite an appreciable number of American citizens should be interested in the life and development of a single English newspaper. That goes to show how close we all are to each other, how innumerable are the strands of which this is but one of the smallest, which bind the two countries together. Yet after all is it so very small? The newspaper to-day plays a tremendous part in the life of all the more advanced nations and perhaps a larger part in Great Britain and America than in any other countries. And undoubtedly we influence each other.

Mostly the influence is from your side to ours, as witness the vast development in the last twenty years of the English popular press formed on American models. But perhaps there are reactions also the other way. We are so like and yet in so many ways so different that we can hardly help having some effect on each other. One great difference between the newspapers of the two countries is that the British ones are more distinctly political and that is largely due to a difference in institutions. If the House of Representatives exercised, besides its own powers, nearly all those also of the Senate and controlled the President, and if besides there were no fixed term to its existence and it might be driven any day to a General Election, what a mighty difference it would make to the day-to-day interest of American domestic politics and what an invasion there would be of the columns of newspapers by political discussion. You would live as it were in a perpetual Presidential election campaign. I do not pretend to say whether this would be an advantage or not, but at least your newspapers would become a good deal more like ours.

Another great difference arises from American isolation. You are so vast, so remote, and so self-contained that the affairs of the outside world tend to lose interest for you. That is changing. You have just taken part in a tremendous European War and you cannot, with the best will in the world, wholly free yourselves from responsibility for its consequences. At this moment * you are engaged in the closing scenes of a great international conference in your capital, by

* Written January 1922.

far the greatest peaceful conference which has ever been held and likely to be the most important and fruitful in its outcome. That brings you again in a responsible way right up against the facts of the world situation. Your newspapers are full of it. They will never again be able quite to empty themselves.

So we are getting nearer to each other, not only in our press but in our peoples. The World is shrinking. Space is every day being bridged. Already we can telegraph through the air or the ether, from Penzance to Melbourne and to-morrow we shall be able to talk by the same mechanism. Physical boundaries are disappearing; moral boundaries must speedily follow suit. The English-speaking peoples should then be quite a comfortable family, gathered as it were round a common hearth.

What a change for the world! What a chance for the newspaper! More and more we shall take our pulpit seriously and preach to all the world. The "Manchester Guardian" has just celebrated its century of more or less creditable existence. May the American reader of this memorial volume be kind to our faults and believe that we live in hopes of correcting at least some of them!

One thought recurs in looking back over these hundred years. During all that great space of time the two countries, though they have had their tiffs and seen rather dangerous ones, have never struck a blow in anger. Now they are closer to each other than ever since the day they parted. Washington has shown that; the settlement with Ireland has confirmed it. That Treaty will stand; it is among the memorable events of history. No man can tell what the future may hold for the relations of the two countries, but, whatever may have been ill done in the past, this surely has been well done and will help to sweeten the whole future. My own recollection goes back over the long years since Mr. Gladstone introduced his first Home Rule Bill, the best and bravest of the three. I have no hesitation in saying that the settlement now reached is better, because it is more complete, than any of those previously attempted. My only regret is for the things that have happened in between, for the continuance of repression, above all for the latest extremes of violence, for the useless addition to the sum of things which history must reprobate and then must seek to forget. It is as the crowning achievement in a long struggle that it appealed first and foremost to the mind of the statesman who has carried it through. I met him a few hours after the Treaty had been signed. "To think that our long struggle is over!" That expressed his thought as it did mine. It is not in Ireland and England alone that there will be relief.

C. P. Scott.

I : *A YOUNG MAN IN A YOUNG CITY*

CHAPTER I

A Young Man in a Young City

§ I

IF we go back to the origin of a newspaper which was established a hundred years ago we shall most likely find ourselves in a commotion of human affairs. Its origin is almost certain to have been volcanic, and we shall discover that it was projected into the world by a storm.

The reasons which suggest and encourage the establishment of a newspaper to-day did not exist a hundred years ago. In our times news is as saleable and merchantable a commodity as soap. It is the only valuable thing in the world which grows everywhere of its own accord. There is not a monarchy or a republic in the world in which it is not being produced day by day and every day ; nor is there a street or a house about us in which it might not spring up suddenly in wild profusion. It is at once as common as the sands and as valuable as fine gold. It is a kind of mineral wealth, and progress has consisted not so much in creating as in unearthing it. Morning by morning and week by week there was quite as much to be told about the world one hundred years ago as there is to-day. The coal was always underneath the valleys, and we have merely sunk the shafts. Journalism, also, has developed on these lines ; it has bored

3

through to the Antipodes. It lifts out of the invisible and the inaudible the fuel and nourishment of an enormous universal curiosity. It has become one of the great providing industries of the world.

Two great movements of recent years have united to bring this about. One of them is mechanical invention, and the other is popular education. It has become possible to collect news from all parts of the country and of the world as though there were no such thing as space ; to print it and even to illustrate it as though there were hardly such a thing as time, and to circulate it among vast numbers of people, most of whom are trained to a high state of, at any rate, superficial curiosity and all of them able to read. One hundred years ago journalism had no advantages such as these. The first number of the *Manchester Guardian* appeared on May 5, 1821, and it happens curiously that its first issue coincided to the day and almost to the hour with one of the most interesting and provocative events in human history. This was the death of Napoleon at St. Helena on May 5, 1821. The world is still greedy, after one hundred years, for any new detail of that wonderful last phase. Could the event occur again, were it known that such an event were pending within the four quarters of the world, modern journalism would station itself like a cat in front of the aperture, and wait for it, rapt and quivering. We look in vain through the first issues of the *Manchester*

4

Guardian for any account of the death of Napoleon. When it is at last mentioned, we find it not announced, but alluded to as something which had got into the public consciousness without the aid of the newspapers. The fact was in the world and journalism knew it not. It was there, but it could not be reached through the envelope of time and space. The opening of that envelope has transformed journalism ; brought into it many with whom it tends to be rather a trade than a calling ; secularized it and possibly materialized it not a little.

But if we return to the origin of a newspaper established a century ago we shall find ourselves among the things of the mind and spirit. Among movements ! Among martyrdoms ! A newspaper in that age had much soul and very little substance. It was most probably established, not to make money, but to make opinion. It had something to say but very little to tell. It thought much more than it knew. It was printed laboriously by hand, and if its opinions were in advance of its times it was edited in dire peril of the law. The *Manchester Guardian* was born in this age of journalism. It was born of the spirit of its age. Its roots bring up much soil of genuine, significant history. It had its origin in imputed heresy and schism and in the struggle of thought to be free. We could no more account for its beginning without reference to the political history of the English people than we could explain the origin of its near neighbour the Cross Street Chapel without entering on the history of religious thought.

§ II

At the beginning of the last century there was living in Hulme, then a rural suburb of Manchester, a certain John Taylor, the proprietor of what was called a classical academy for boys. This John Taylor came of a family which had settled at Stand, near to Manchester, and he was himself educated at the Stand Grammar School. The village of Stand is still distinguished by an historic Unitarian chapel, and John Taylor, being associated with its congregation, entered the Unitarian ministry, and was appointed to the charge of a congregation at Ilminster, in Somersetshire. The church at Ilminster seems to have been visited by doubts of the spirit. The Rev. John Taylor reconsidered his thinking, with the result that he left the Unitarian body, removed with his wife, who was a religious poetess of some note, to Bristol, where he engaged in scholastic work, and finally settled in Manchester, the school which he opened in Hulme enjoying the patronage of the Society of Friends, and he himself being now numbered among the Quakers.

To John Taylor, while still acting as a Unitarian minister at Ilminster, was born in 1791 a son, John Edward Taylor, who grew up to be one of the early reformers, to give powerful aid to the people in the affair of Peterloo, to suffer himself in the cause of reform, and to find along this dark and stormy path the final purpose of his life in the establishment of the *Manchester Guardian*. John Edward Taylor spent a studious youth at his father's house in Islington Street, Salford. At the age of fifteen he was having lessons in mathematics twice a week from John Dalton, the scientist, who was teaching in Faulkner Street. When the time came for him to begin life for himself he was put to join a manufacturer of the name of Oakden, and in this business he rose steadily and rapidly from the status of an apprentice to that of a partner. While he was still a youth Joseph Lancaster began to travel the country to explain and expound the methods of teaching poor children which he had adopted at the famous school in the Borough Road, London. Earnest people in many parts of the country formed Lancasterian schools to supply the almost complete absence of popular education, and of one of these Lancasterian schools, which speedily drifted into deep theological waters and was torn by the secession from its Committee of all the Socinian members, John Edward Taylor became the secretary.

Glimpses are possible to us of the domestic life in Islington Street, Salford—the father an anxious navigator among the metaphysics who had already travelled from Unitarianism to Quakerism, and was now drifting to Swedenborgianism ; the mother dead ; the only sister away on a round of visits among Dissenting

7

friends and connections, and the young John Edward Taylor finding something short of complete diversion in the undiluted company of the theologian. " Even a well-furnished table," we hear of him saying, " is unsatisfactory without a woman at it." The father seems to have felt this too. " But with these things (the troubles at the Lancasterian School caused by the Socinian members) it is not necessary," he writes to his daughter, " while thou art at this distance to trouble thee, but on these and many other accounts I want the comfort of thy company, and so does Edward. We had last evening (February 4, 1812) B. Oakden to drink tea with us, and his wife and niece, which last came near an hour before the others, and I could not help admiring how comfortable it seemed to have a female about the house."

John Edward Taylor was, however, finding many interests in the town. He was a member of the Junior Literary and Philosophical Society. He paid occasional visits to London, and his interest in the Liberal movement of the day is shown in a visit which he paid while in London to Leigh Hunt, who, having narrowly and chiefly by the merits of Henry Brougham's advocacy, escaped punishment for an article on the savagery of military floggings, was now, when John Edward Taylor called on him, undergoing two years' imprisonment for describing the Prince Regent as " a corpulent man of fifty, a libertine over head and ears in disgrace, a man who has just closed half a century without one single claim on the gratitude of his country or the respect of posterity." John Edward Taylor writes to his sister an account of his visit to Leigh Hunt, " a very interesting and agreeable young man, and, all things considered, quite as comfortable as can be expected in prison " ; encloses a copy of Lord Byron's *Giaour* (just out) ; announces his intention of staying another night in London to be present at Covent Garden, and concludes by hoping that his father " is in good health and (what is perhaps of more consequence) good humour." A very sprightly letter ! It was about this time, 1812 or 1813, that John Edward Taylor, notwithstanding that he was doing well in the cotton business, in which his exact functions were those of a " chapman," began to find his main interest in politics and formed the habit of contributing paragraphs to the Manchester press. Like Leigh Hunt, he was destined to find Liberal journalism in the early years of the nineteenth century a perilous game.

The early reformers in Manchester went in fear of their lives from two sides. On the one side was the magistrate ; on the other, the mob. From the outbreak of the French Revolution in 1789 until a period which we may fix about the year 1812 there was in Manchester an informal but effective co-operation between law and disorder against the few men who stood out for liberal ideas. In 1792 these men formed

9

the " Manchester Constitutional Society." In the membership we find the names of Thomas Walker, James Darbishire, George Lloyd, Thomas Cooper (a barrister), George Philips (afterwards Sir George Philips), and Thomas Kershaw. The Society aimed at altering by peaceful means a representative system which allowed two members of Parliament to Old Sarum, which was an empty field, and denied a voice in the government of the country to great cities like Manchester and Birmingham. Twelve years before the Constitutional Society was formed, its opinions had enjoyed the open support of William Pitt, and at the trial of Horne Tooke, in 1794, William Pitt was called as a witness for the defence to say that the doctrines and practices of the reformers of 1794 were precisely those which he himself had held in 1780.

But in the meantime the French Revolution had occurred. William Pitt, the pupil of Adam Smith and the young hope of Liberalism, was now, as Prime Minister, fighting, at once on the battlefields of Europe and in the police courts of England, with subsidies abroad and with spies at home, a war against all opinion which was not the opinion of George III. The Reign of Terror began. Louis XVI. was executed, and George III. feared that " if a stop was not put to French principles there would not be a king left in Europe in a few years." All Europe shivered with horror at such deeds. Highly residential Mosley Street shivered, and the several orders of Manchester society, the men of the law and the men of the Gospel, the Boroughreeve and constables, and the Fellows of the Collegiate Church, whom we should now call the Canons of the Cathedral, joined together in the process known as nipping it in the bud.

Tsarism began. Its chief instrument was Joseph Nadin, the deputy constable, an official whose broad Lancashire dialect, great physical girth and sallow face, and the heavy, illiterate hand which he brought to bear on the fine points of what a man had said and what he had meant, have won for him a permanent place among the characters of gaolership, though it is fair to add that Samuel Bamford, the weaver-poet, found something in the man which he did not wholly dislike. To every weaver in Manchester who had on his conscience so much as a single visit to a political club " Mesthur Nadin " was a name of terror. The principles which actuated him as a public official are summarized in an extract from his professional talk to a political prisoner whom he was conducting from Middleton to Manchester. " Ween larn thee," he said in the carriage on the way to the New Bailey prison, " ween larn thee to be a Jacobin." And so they did ! The members of the Manchester Constitutional Society were marked men. In 1794 Thomas Walker was tried at the Lancaster Assizes on an indictment of conspiracy with others to overthrow the Constitution and Government. The spy who was the principal witness against him broke down completely under cross-examination, and the jury returned a verdict of not guilty. But the terms in which the judge dismissed the prisoner from the dock show clearly that the affair had gone near to hang him. The early reformers were broken up. They were too far in advance of their times. Some went ɟo live in Liverpool. Others ceased to be Whigs. Life in the town was, in fact, unbearable for a Whig.

For these exertions of the magistrates and the spies had about them one quality which we should not expect. They were on the whole popular measures. They reflected the sentiment of the town. Manchester was not at this time, and never has been throughout its history, a Whig city. It has nothing like the Whig record of the City of London or the City of Westminster or that of Birmingham. In 1745 it was a Jacobite town, devoted to " legitimism " and the divine right of kings, burning torches below the bed-chamber of the foolish Pretender, whose headquarters in the city can still be faintly traced in the name of " Palace Street," off Market Street. Exactly one hundred years later —in 1845—the town was on the eve of winning the great triumph of thought and will which placed it among the intellectually illustrious cities of the world. But the argument which was coming to its tremendous close in 1845 was economic, and the statesman who translated the will of Manchester into an Act of Parliament was a Conservative. The Manchester School was a school of economic thinking. Between the dates 1745 and 1845 the city had reacted, and, since then and down to present times, it has continued to react on the whole unfavourably to Whig and Liberal tests. It dismissed Bright. It was never Gladstonian, and in our own times of 1906, when it once again for a few moments led the Liberal thinking of England, the issue before the country was an economic one.

It was this state of popular sentiment—the *vox populi*—rather than the severity of the magistrate or the industry of the spy which crushed the early reformers among whom John Edward Taylor's boyhood was spent. The people voted steadily for Barabbas. In 1793 Pitt had declared the war against French principles which was to last on and off for twenty-two years ; which made and had to be continued till it unmade Napoleon ; which cost us twelve hundred millions sterling, and ended by restoring the Bourbons to France and saddling England with a corn law which caused the country thirty years of semi-starvation. In Manchester the war was very popular. The fathers had lost nights of sleep for " Prince Charlie " and the divine right of kings, and the sons now proceeded to sustain themselves body and soul on military glory and to be richly blessed with the spectacle of men marching and counter-marching on Kersal Moor. The Whig reformers, who were opposed to the war, became " the friends of the enemy." They were " pro-French," just as Burke a few years before had been a " pro-American." Being " pro-French," they were excommunicated from the town.

The method of excommunication was simple. Manchester in those days circulated around its inns and taverns and public-houses, of which in 1793 there were 186. To understand the excommunication of Liberal opinion we have to understand that in those days there was no drink question. Drink was not a question at all, but an axiom or a postulate, and that hardly less among Nonconformists than in the circles of Church and King. It will indeed be remembered that some of the staunchest pillars of the early Evangelicals, and of the Clapham set in which Macaulay was brought up, were brewers, and rather proud of it. There were in English society in those days none of those concentrations of purpose on single ends which we call " causes " or " fads," according as we subscribe to them or not. The first of the long and diversified procession of " causes " was the movement for the abolition of slavery. The temperance movement did not begin till towards the thirties of the last century, though Henry Hunt, the orator of Peterloo, had before this period inculcated total abstinence and caused it to spread among his Radical followers mainly as a method of depriving an aristocratic and arbitrary Government of its revenue. Accordingly, when the 186 publicans and innkeepers of Manchester joined together in a solemn pledge to refuse the custom of " the daring miscreants whose object it was to assist the French savages," under which form of words (drawn up for them by one of the Collegiate Church clergy) they were understood without ambiguity to be referring to the Whig party of Manchester, they pronounced a sentence of all but social extinction. As late as 1825 there was on a wall of a public-house in Bridge Street a board bearing the words " No Jacobins admitted here," but in that year the tide of opinion had turned, and the board, which was not so much a board as a mural tablet, was removed.

The people backed up these measures against the peace party with energetic undertakings of their own. They " said ditto to Mr. Burke." The doors of Cross Street Chapel were hammered in with trees rooted up in St. Ann's Square in the belief that that building was a nest of pacifism, which indeed it was. Before the close of the eighteenth century a Liberal newspaper had been established by Mr. Matthew Faulkner. It was called the *Manchester Herald*, and it made a spirited defence of Liberal principles for about eighteen months, at the end of which period the mob forcibly put it down and wrecked the printing office in Market Place. Those who stood up for the cause of the people did well in these days to keep their windows boarded up.

§ III

But a change of opinion was coming. Prices were rising. Wheat, which had been 6*s.* a bushel before the war, was costing 16*s.* 8*d.* a bushel in 1801, and bread riots began to occur. In 1807 the famous Orders in Council declared all the French dominions in a state of blockade. After the fashion of these economic weapons, the measure proved rather sharper at the handle than at the point, and its effect was the almost complete destruction of our commerce abroad. The mercantile classes began to show some uneasiness, and the Manchester weavers, whose wages were said to average 7*s.* a week in weeks of full employment, took to holding riotous meetings in favour of a minimum wage. At one of these meetings in St. George's Fields in 1808 the 4th Dragoon Guards were called out, and one of the weavers was killed and several wounded. Colonel Hanson, of Strangeways Hall, the "weavers' friend," an attractive though somewhat ineffectual figure, makes his brief transit of the public stage, and William Cobbett began to teach a receptive people a doubtful political economy in unexceptionable English. In 1812 the popular temper had so far altered that a loyal meeting called to welcome Castlereagh and Sidmouth to high office in the Government provoked a counter-demonstration which, getting out of hand, led in its turn to the sensational burning of the Royal Exchange. This incident was taken as showing that the days of the " Church and King " mob were at an end and that the ice which had locked down every form of dissentient political opinion was breaking up.

From this time forward we begin to hear the gathering voice of the people ; some crying one thing and some another ; one party calling for factory legislation ; another making audible certain abstruse reasons for blaming the currency ; a third busy night by night breaking machinery and burning ricks ; yet another asking already for a repeal of the bread taxes, and a small preoccupied section inflamed chiefly by tithes and church rates, until all these voices joined and finally became irresistible in the general cry of the middle and working class for reform, the *sine qua non* of every hope and plan and cure for the ills of the times.

For the burning of the Exchange the writer of a placard " Now or Never " which had been posted on the walls of the town was held chiefly responsible. The authorship of this manifesto was doubtfully attributed to John Edward Taylor, now a young man of twenty-one, and we shall see this charge, repeated seven years later, giving rise to a trial of some importance to politics and journalism at the Lancaster Assizes. That the placard should between the years 1812 and 1819 have been generally attributed to him in the Tory gossip of the town is an indication of the rise of his importance between these two years. New times were coming and, with the new times, new men. The dynastic names of Philips and

17

Potter and Greg and Absolom Watkin and Rylands are found occurring in the reported transactions of the time. Liberalism and Dissent were beginning to breed the makings of the Manchester school of politics, and Unitarianism in particular was preparing to flower into families of powerful and accomplished citizenship. And as Napoleonic Manchester follows Jacobite Manchester into impalpability and the ancestry of modern men and the origination of modern things comes into sight ; as the way, though still long and painful and with Peterloo a landmark still to be reached and passed, begins nevertheless to open out towards enfranchisement and municipalization ; as the last reluctant handloom weavers are drawn into the factory system —in this early dawn of our own times, when every year saw some event, some business founded or some movement launched on its way, which is now blossoming into centenary—in these days of small things that were to last and grow, we find John Edward Taylor actively shaping the events of his times and town, and, what is more to the point, being decisively shaped by events himself.

He was now in business as a Manchester merchant for himself. He lived in his father's house in Islington Street, Salford, and addressed his business lettters from Toll Lane Buildings, but his thoughts were more and more occupied with the Whig politics of the time. He had found his own means of service to the cause of

18

reform as a pamphleteer. He was the most active and industrious of a small band of young men who seized on the local journalism of Manchester and made the first beginnings in transforming what had been a mere hole-and-corner industry of scissors and paste, varied by an occasional antic of scurrility, into an instrument for the systematic statement of views and the winning of purpose.

The man by whose goodwill the first experiments in pure journalism were made in Manchester was William Cowdroy. John Edward Taylor and his friends, among whom we must include Archibald Prentice, the spiritual father of the *Manchester Examiner*, were now writing articles week by week in the Whig interest in *Cowdroy's Manchester Gazette*. About the end of the eighteenth and the beginning of the nineteenth centuries Manchester saw many newspapers come and go. It was one of the signs of ferment. We have seen how the *Manchester Herald*, established as a Liberal organ in 1792, was forcibly suppressed by the mob in the following year. Another Radical paper, the *Manchester Observer*, was in existence in 1819, and one of its printers, Mr. Saxton, was included in the band who went to prison with Henry Hunt for the affair of Peterloo. Among the Tory newspapers of the time we find a greater tenacity of life. Wheeler's *Manchester Chronicle* and Harrop's *Mercury*, two ultra-Tory organs, were refusing to receive Whig advertisements or to print news of the Whig party as early as 1792, and were both still in existence in 1825. In the same proprietorship with Harrop's *Mercury* was Harrop's *British Volunteer*, a paper whose bones were afterwards built, as we shall see, into the fabric of the *Manchester Guardian*. The *Exchange Herald*, owned by an amiable citizen named Aston, ranked as a Conservative paper. It had, however, done an important service to liberty in 1810 by printing a letter which helped materially to arouse Nonconformists to the dangers of Lord Sidmouth's Dissenters Bill and set them petitioning vigorously against a measure which, if it had not been withdrawn, would have required every preacher not in connection with the Established Church to provide himself with a testimonial from six persons deemed by a magistrate, who might be clerically-minded and might even be actually a cleric, to be " substantial and reputable."

It was reserved to *Cowdroy's Manchester Gazette* among this numerous band of contemporaries to leave its traces on the politics and journalism of the nineteenth century, and indeed it would be possible to show that this newspaper is the root from which all the subsequent journalism of Manchester has directly or derivatively sprung. *Cowdroy's Manchester Gazette* began to be published in St. Mary's Gate about the year 1795, and it reached the height of its career about 1816, when William Cowdroy, a man of character and wit and a writer himself much to the taste of the town, had begun to accept the voluntary assistance in his columns of John Edward Taylor, Archibald Prentice, and others, and to brave the serious risks to which such young men would be constantly exposing him in such times of prosecution for seditious libel. " Are you not afraid," Prentice once asked him, " of an indictment for this ? " " Not I," said Cowdroy ; " write away." It was the gay, courageous, and liberal spirit of this forgotten worthy, half-compositor and half-editor, satirical writer who set up his own lampoons in type, which gave Manchester its first experience of a critical, watchful, and outspoken press.

II : *THE BIRTH OF A NEWSPAPER*

CHAPTER II

The Birth of a Newspaper

§ I

THESE early beginnings of the local press had grown large enough by 1819 to enable it to play a considerable part in the affair of Peterloo. If we wish to reconstruct the crime of Peterloo we shall have to imagine a modern Whit-Monday on August 16, 1819. The procession which went through the streets of Manchester was in its Sunday clothes. It included many women and children, and though the object of the demonstration was to demand the extension of the franchise the day widened out into a popular holiday. From early morning little local processions were coming into Manchester, tributaries of the great stream of people which ultimately went through the streets with bands playing and banners flying, and collected on the site of the present Free Trade Hall. We can see how wide a stretch of country had drained itself into Manchester from the circumstance that of the persons killed by the swords of the yeomanry only a minority were actually of Manchester, the others coming from Oldham, Chadderton, Saddleworth, Eccles, Hyde, and Barton. The procession went past the drawing-room windows of Mosley Street, and when it had poured on to the place of meeting on St. Peter's Field the town assumed for half an hour that drained and bloodless aspect which is proper to Sunday afternoon but comes at other times of all the circulation of the town having rushed to one place.

At the end of this brief period all the main roads out of Manchester were streaming with panic. A witness to the events of the day, who did not indeed see the central event on St. Peter's Field, tells how he was coming into the town by way of Chapel Street, Salford, and met people running in the direction of Pendleton, " their faces pale as death and some with blood trickling down their cheeks." It was with difficulty that he could get anyone to stop and tell him what had happened.

It is soon told. The magistrates were watching the proceedings from a convenient window. They had formed the decision to arrest Hunt in the face of the whole assemblage. To assist in this enterprise they had at their command all the special constables of the town, two hundred additional special constables sworn in for the occasion, and a mixed military force of cavalry, yeomanry, artillery, and infantry, which was kept concealed behind a neighbouring wall. It is a significant thing that the privilege of striking the first blow at the defenceless crowd was entrusted not to the cavalry but to the yeomanry, which was a local force and was indeed the quintessence of local Toryism. The yeomanry drove their horses headlong into the crowd. The crowd did not resist them, but its great size and

A CONTEMPORARY IMPRESSION OF PETERLOO.

its inertness all but smothered them. In a few minutes the yeomanry were no longer a compact and concerted force but a number of widely divided men, stuck in the crowd like raisins in a pudding—blindly hitting out. The 15th Hussars were sent in to their rescue.

It was soon over, and we are now to imagine St. Peter's Field an empty and deserted acre, strewn with caps and bonnets and hats and Lancashire shawls ; the dead lying about in this débris ; the yeomanry dismounted and easing their horses' girths ; special constables talking among themselves ; all the blinds drawn at windows which looked upon the scene. After an attack with swords the wounded are in a high proportion to the dead. Eleven persons were killed. Some 560 wounded, of whom 140 were severely wounded, came before the committee which raised a subscription for the relief of suffering, and many more nursed their broken heads at home for fear of confessing that they had taken part in a demonstration the object of which was to demand a voice in the government of the country for grown men and great cities.

Among the people on the platform who were arrested with Henry Hunt was a certain Mr. Tyas, the reporter for the *Times*. It was this Mr. Tyas who introduced into his report of a speech by Lord Brougham a long and not inappropriate passage of Cicero. He meant it as a valuable offering to the great orator and was much surprised when Lord Brougham, who had not quoted the passage and happened to be unfamiliar with it, treated its introduction as an unwarrantable liberty. The *Times* was doing great service at this period to the independence of journalism and to the Liberal movement, and it is evidence at once of a high public spirit and of some professional enterprise that it should have sent a reporter to the meeting which was to be addressed by Henry Hunt. Peterloo is the début of the reporter in English public life. To the local community of the press it was no small matter that the *Times* reporter had dropped down among them, and the full reports which the *Times* afterwards gave of Hunt's trial at Lancaster originated, through emulation, the practice of the art of reporting in Manchester. Spending the night of Peterloo in prison, Mr. Tyas was momentarily put out of journalistic action, but the account of the affair which he sent to the *Times* on his release and the evidence he gave at Hunt's trial are important historical testimony against the magistrates. The reformers greatly feared that, with Mr. Tyas in prison, the magisterial party would get the first access to the ear of the country, and it was in preventing this calamity that the journalistic " hand " of John Edward Taylor came into important use.

On the evening of the same day John Edward Taylor wrote a full account of the occurrence to a London paper. Archibald Prentice, who was not only Taylor's colleague on the *Gazette* but his next-door neighbour in Islington Street,

Salford, wrote a full account for another paper. Both narratives left Manchester by the night coach, and, appearing in print within some forty-eight hours of the affair, got ahead of and were never overtaken by the official version. Mr. Tyas, on his release, corroborated Taylor and Prentice, and added damaging details of his own. Other newspapers helped. Mr. John Smith, of the *Liverpool Mercury*, and Mr. Edward Baines, jun., of the *Leeds Mercury*, had both been present, and it was mainly owing to Liberal journalism that Peterloo brought a great mass of middle-class and aristocratic opinion over to the cause of reform. The magistrates and the military might be thanked by the Government ; Sidmouth might carry his " Six Acts " to stamp out sedition by dint of fine, imprisonment, or banishment for life ; the Rev. W. R. Hay, magistrate and cleric, might receive the living of Rochdale and its emoluments of £2400 a year for his services in " putting down " reformers and reform. But it was in vain. Peterloo brought the Reform Bill much nearer. It lifted the Whig party miles and years on the way towards the combined triumph and collapse of 1832.

§ II

By this time John Edward Taylor was contemplating and was perhaps preparing for the establishment of a newspaper of his own. He was now literary man in chief to the Whig party of Manchester. It was he who wrote the manifesto of the party in a pamphlet which is still a standard authority for the affair of Peterloo. Still more to the point, he had already made his own journey along that road to Lancaster which had been trod by Thomas Walker, Henry Hunt, and Samuel Bamford—the "Via Dolorosa" of Lancashire reformers. He had been in peril of the law. The prosecution of John Edward Taylor for libel arose out of that placard "Now or Never" which had been thought the immediate cause of the burning of the Royal Exchange in 1812. In July, 1818, there was a meeting of the police commissioners in Salford for the purpose of appointing the assessors, a body which performed certain rudimentary duties of local government. The name of John Edward Taylor was in the list of eligible assessors, and when it was reached a certain Mr. Gill asked, "Who is this Mr. Taylor?" Mr. John Greenwood, who appears to have been presiding, replied that Mr. Taylor was one of the reformers who went about the country making speeches. Mr. Joseph Brotherton, who lived at this time in a country cottage in Oldfield Lane but became afterwards the first Liberal member for Salford and made some figure in the House of Commons, said that Mr. Taylor would not make a worse assessor for being a politician. If Mr. Taylor was a reformer, Mr. Brotherton added, he was a moderate one. "Moderate indeed," Mr. Greenwood replied; "he was the author of the handbill that caused the Manchester Exchange to be set on fire in 1812." Mr. Taylor's name was accordingly passed over.

John Edward Taylor was greatly stung by this attack. He made repeated applications to Mr. Greenwood for the withdrawal of the charge. He thought of challenging Mr. Greenwood to a duel, and finally, obtaining no satisfaction, he wrote to Mr. Greenwood describing him as " a liar, a slanderer, and a scoundrel," published the letter by placing a copy of it at the office of *Cowdroy's Gazette* for general inspection, and was as the result indicted for a criminal libel at the Lancaster Assizes in March, 1819, the trial having been removed there from the Salford Quarter Sessions.

The trial at Lancaster is notable for the inroad it made on the doctrine of the courts that the truth of the statement complained of was no defence to an indictment for libel ; that the truth of the libel constituted, in fact, an aggravation of the charge. John Edward Taylor managed through the vacillation of the counsel for the prosecution to call evidence that Greenwood had in fact slandered him, and that he and not Greenwood was the person aggrieved. In a spirited address to the jury he protested against truth being visited with the penalties of falsehood. With Baron Wood on the bench, with Scarlett (afterwards Lord Abinger) leading for the prosecution, and all but a dozen loyalists in the box, the defence would never have worked but for the accident that John Rylands, of Warrington, was the foreman of the jury. John Rylands prevented the jury from giving a verdict without leaving the box. He insisted on retiring. He kept the jury in retirement so long that when the verdict was at length agreed on it had to be communicated to the judge in bed. John Edward Taylor had been attended all day by a band of devoted friends. One of them described the procession of the jury, the janitors, the prisoner, the prisoner's friends through the narrow streets of Lancaster to the judge's lodgings on a windy night ; the lantern going on ahead ; the squeezing of the whole crowd into a moderate-sized bedroom ; the judge in bed ; the judge's nightcap.

John Rylands pronounced the verdict. If he had not out-argued the jury he had out-stayed them and out-starved them. The verdict was " Not guilty." The room, the lobby outside the room, the staircase and the street outside rang with the cheers of Taylor's friends. The next morning he was formally acquitted in court, and he left Lancaster about noon on his return to Manchester. One of his attendants to Lancaster had been Mr. John Childs, of Bungay, in the county of Suffolk, a printer and a personage in the history of Bible printing. He was not so much a friend of Mr. Taylor's as a friend of a friend, but he had got into the inner ring of the affair and was contributing much in admiration and sympathy. " It is now plain," the enthusiastic Mr. Childs said to Mr. Taylor in the coach on the way home, " it is now plain you have the elements of public work in you ; why don't you set up a newspaper ? " To these words the *Manchester Guardian* owes its birth.

The project matured for two years, and while it was maturing John Edward Taylor abandoned the idea he had been entertaining of going to the Bar. The proprietors of the *Leeds Mercury* and the *Liverpool Mercury* were consulted, and were found full of encouragement and hope. *Cowdroy's Gazette* was known by now to draw much of its value from the part which John Edward Taylor was gratuitously taking in its columns, and for a time it seemed probable that *Cowdroy's* night be purchased and made worthier of the growing party of Whigs and Reformers and of the " populous and in-telligent district," as Mr. Taylor put it, " in which we are situated." But Mr. Cowdroy refused to sell, and the project for establishing an entirely new paper was resumed. In the end the sum of £1000 was raised in more or less equal contributions by some twelve friends of Mr. Taylor, all of them Whigs and Reformers and most of them Unitarians, and this sum formed the capital on which the *Manchester Guardian* began its career. The money was subscribed under an agreement that if the experiment failed each of the twelve contributors was to regard his subscription as lost ; if it succeeded each was to be repaid. The agreement was creditable to all parties and it was faithfully observed.

But there is no doubt that while the bargain gave a decisive turn to John Edward Taylor's career and carried him out of business into professional journalism, its precise terms determined also to some extent the kind of journalist he was to be. He was anxious to justify the confidence of his friends, and in the effort to do this he became much more absorbed than had been expected in the technique of journalism. Some of his backers expected a weekly tract for the times. They got, instead, a tractarianism much milder than that which continued to issue week by week from the office of the *Gazette*. But with it they obtained much the best newspaper Manchester had yet known. It had been usual in the Manchester papers to dismiss the most important meeting in a paragraph—" A large meeting was held in the Bull's Head on Thursday last, for the resolutions of which see advertisement in our front page." The *Guardian* was the first paper in Manchester to employ a professional reporter who performs the characteristic functions of journalism. It was less shrill than the current journalism of the town and more orchestrated. The prospectus, which is from the hand of John Edward Taylor, and a favourable example of English prose as it was the day after Gibbon and the day but one after Johnson, promises that the accompaniment to the main political theme of journalism shall not be neglected, and that it will indeed be somewhat developed by systematic attention to literature and science, by foreign intelligence, and what we might call the secular news of the town and district.

§ III

We need constantly to correct our perspective in taking the account of past times from the historian. If we forgot to do this we should suppose that human life in Manchester from 1821 till 1846 consisted in nothing but violently rushing to and fro, in assembling or dispersing, in being furiously a Whig or a Tory or a Cobdenite, as the case may be. But this is a mistake, and on all except perhaps twenty-five days at the most in those twenty-five years the ordinary people of Manchester were probably as little conscious of the beat and rhythm of public history as the little fishes we see on the surface of the river are aware that they are living in flowing water, and that the rapids are just round the bend in the journey and experience of the stream.

It is true the Corn Law of 1815 imposed throughout this period a ceaseless pressure on the growing frame of the town, but society, like the individual, has a private life which continues in almost any state of politics. In the darkest political days of the early nineteenth century Edmund Kean is acting Othello or Sir Giles Overreach, and William Hazlitt lecturing on poetry, and the audiences assisting at these events are large. George IV sets a perplexing new fashion of sea-bathing and in Manchester people begin to go by coach to Southport to indulge this strange new fad, the journey occupying five hours. "The Rivals" is given at the Theatre Royal to introduce Mrs. Davison, Mr. Johnstone, and Mr. W. Farren, but "the house was not so full as might have been expected from the celebrity of these performers." The *Guardian* is somewhat severe on the performance submitted by "Mr. F." It is believed in Scottish literary circles that "Mrs. Grant, the author of *Letters from the Mountains*, is also the author of *Waverley* and other fashionable novels so generally ascribed to Sir Walter Scott." The *Guardian* places before its readers some of the evidence adduced in support of this theory, but does not commit itself either way. "On Monday evening a young man passing down the narrow part of Market Street was very severely injured by being crushed between the wall and the wheel of a carrier's cart." A few days later the bells of the Collegiate Church are rung all through Thursday in honour of the passing of the Manchester Streets Bill, which will empower the town to widen Market Street and so prevent such dreadful accidents for the future. So life proceeds, beyond the power of politics to hinder or help !

Even in its earliest numbers we see the editor of the *Guardian* trying to be more things to more men than Mr. Harrop ever attempted to be in the *Mercury*, which was often little more

36

than scraps of transplanted poetry and the local dog fights, or than Mr. Cowdroy had thought it his journalistic duty to be in the *Gazette*. We begin through the *Guardian* to hear the speaker at the meeting and to see the actor on the stage. We are with the prisoner at his trial, and not infrequently, in the hard spirit of the age, we accompany him with glued eyes every inch of the way to the scaffold. We read that a certain prisoner has, owing to the special and peculiar quality of her crime, to be dragged to the place of execution on a hurdle, and as she approaches the end of her journey her cries are so sustained and shrill that every countenance in the large company of spectators " is struck into an aspect of dismay." The thing begins to be a mirror of the times. It was, again, much the handsomest paper that had come out of the town. We find it almost from the beginning climbing on to the knee of the cotton trade and talking, again, about the currency which was being much injured by the issue of local notes, and whereas Mr. Wheeler of the *Chronicle* would not look at an advertisement after one o'clock on Friday, the *Guardian* obliged the public by accepting revenue until the very moment of going to press.

From this time forward the life of John Edward Taylor belongs much more to journalism and much less to politics. His opinions did not change and he remained a moderate Whig, though he is said to have become in later life a Malthusian and, like most of the early Mal-

37

thusians, to have largely given up hope. Archibald Prentice, who also began a public career by writing for *Cowdroy's Gazette*, and who was to spend a literary lifetime in the service first of reform and afterwards of the League, blames his early friend severely for an increasing absorption in the temporalities of journalism, and deplores the speedy gravitation of the *Guardian* from " the Left " in politics to a position near to " the Centre," and not always clearly distinguishable from " the Right." He complains of too much " management " of public questions and a certain " steersmanship." But the drama is not in three acts or even in five. The services which the *Manchester Guardian* was able to render in later years to the minority in English politics would not have been performed with so much effect, and perhaps could not have been performed at all, if it had not been deeply versed in the full technique of journalism, a powerful, efficient, and familiar newspaper, trusted unreservedly for the facts. It began to acquire this character and to build it up under the cautious, catholic, unsensational editorship of John Edward Taylor. First the natural body and then the spiritual !

III : *IN THE DAYS OF SMALL THINGS*

CHAPTER III

In the Days of Small Things

§ I

THE *Manchester Guardian* of May 5, 1821, was a four-page paper of 24 columns. It appeared once a week, went to press on Friday evening, and was formally issued to the world on Saturday. Its most striking physical feature was the crimson Revenue stamp impressed in the top right-hand corner of its front page. The stamp was an object not undecorative in itself, but it indicated, especially when we remember that there was in addition to it an unseen but potent tax of 3*s.* 6*d.* on each advertisement and a duty of 3*d.* a pound on paper, a severe drag on the possible commercial progress of the undertaking. It was the Revenue stamp which entered most heavily into the price of the paper. Of the 7*d.* charged for each copy 4*d.* was paid to the Government as a tax on knowledge.

The *Guardian* appeared when the newspaper tax stood at the highest point it ever reached. It had been imposed at a lower rate in the reign of Queen Anne as an instrument for the repression of troublesome opinion, and both Addison and Swift mention the heavy mortality it caused among the newspapers of their day. When it was lowered to a penny in 1836 and finally abolished in 1855 the deportment of society towards the newspaper underwent a marked change. An etiquette disappeared. The stamped newspaper was a means of social ceremony and obligation. Not many people had it, and the man who owned it, owned it to some extent for the benefit of his neighbours, even as a man might own a watering-can or a pair of stepladders or any other article of occasional utility for which he gets known over his garden wall. People presented their compliments to one another and begged to be favoured with a few moments' loan of the *Gazette* or the *Dispatch*. Being borrowed, it was duly returned, or it was passed on by consent to another applicant, but the air and aspect of a private estate which have evaporated out of any morning newspaper of to-day by the time the sun has reached its noonday height would easily hang for a week about the old journal which came down from London by the *Rocket* and contained an important speech by Sir Robert or Lord John. It was property. The owner had what the lawyers call constructive possession of it even when it was out of his hands. A letter written by a Nonconformist minister in 1831 may be quoted for its illustration of a kind of finesse, stylishness, and we might say virtuosity as of a man tasting claret, which is now hopelessly lost to the process and occupation of reading the news of the day, as well for the somewhat beautiful light it throws on the deliberate habits of an age which was vanishing even as he wrote.

I was very glad, he says, to find that you enjoyed your excursion to Manchester by the steam carriage.

42

What a delightful mode of travelling it is! You had 150 fellow-passengers, I find. What a number to travel by the same carriage! What eventful times have I lived to see! Such a plan of Parliamentary reform I never expected to see submitted to Parliament by any ministry as that proposed by Lord John Russell this day week. Mr. Edward Carter was so good as to send me over the *Morning Chronicle*. I found it on my table when I returned home to tea with a message that I would return it when I had done with it. I accordingly read the leading article containing the outlines of the plan, and then hastily looked over Lord John Russell's speech. When I returned it, I borrowed it again the next morning to look at it more leisurely, and then sent it on to Dr. Waller, requesting him to return it to Mr. Carter.

Stamps here and duties there were not the only difficulties in the way of the new enterprise. As a Liberal organ it was born to trouble as the sparks flew upwards. The Government which fleeced also frowned. A Liberal editor edited with the Attorney-General at his elbow, and, lest the Attorney-General should slumber and sleep, there was the London Constitutional Association, a body of amateur censors, on the watch. Finally, the *Guardian* had its own private and peculiar difficulty in the fierce journalistic competition which was raging in the town. The "sevenpenny" public has its definite boundaries even to-day, but one hundred years ago it was extremely limited, and the "sevenpenny" public was already staked out among no fewer than seven newspapers, large and small. *Wheeler's Chronicle*, with a circulation of at least 3000 and secure

43

of the advertising goodwill of the town, was the Goliath of this host.

But there were two departments of journalism in which practically nothing had as yet been done. The one was that of the leader-writer, and the other that of the reporter. For foreign intelligence and for the speeches in Parliament the *Guardian* was dependent, like all its rivals, on its own scissors and paste and the London papers—the *Morning Post*, which Coleridge had recently been making glorious ; the *Times*, a strong Liberal paper in those days ; and the brilliant *Morning Chronicle*, which was so often in trouble for sedition that it was almost edited from Newgate. For district news, again, by which term we should understand news from the towns around Manchester, it was necessary to look to voluntary contributions, and we find the editor begging in his prospectus to be furnished with paragraphs of local interest. The things which were special and peculiar to the *Guardian* for the present were the literary character of John Edward Taylor and the shorthand which Jeremiah Garnett had invented while acting as a printer on *Wheeler's Chronicle*.

John Edward Taylor was the first newspaper proprietor in Manchester who was capable of acting as his own editor, and the first editor in the town who could write. Some attempt had been made, as we have seen, and chiefly by Mr. Taylor himself, to develop the leading article in *Cowdroy's Gazette*. Mr. Wheeler and Mr. Harrop, on their parts, despised it. Even in the *Guardian* it was some years before it acquired its full modern sacrosanctity. In the early numbers we find it abbreviated and even on occasion omitted for want of space. It is more shocking to find it now and then unwritten for want of time, and to catch the editor signing promissory notes to deal with something or other " next week." Many years later—in the days when the Anti-Corn Law League had nearly won but not quite, and the Free Trade Hall was being thrown together with nails and timber so that the great argument could be heard argued out, and the opening speeches of chairmen were stopped while the workmen wrenched boards from the roof for air and breathing—in those missionary days the *Guardian* would allow itself from time to time to be literally swamped by the eloquence of Cobden and Bright, and the leading article would be held over for want of space if not of breath. This was not good journalism, but it was exceptional. From the first the leading article was a feature of the *Guardian*, a new entertainment and a new force in the politics and journalism of the town. The other art by which the paper hoped to make its way was that of the reporter. No other paper in the town had a reporter. The *Guardian* introduced him and his function into the life of Manchester. It introduced him in the person of Jeremiah Garnett.

The first number of the *Guardian* announces that the paper is " printed and published by

J. Garnett at No. 29, Market Street." This is not to be taken as a legal fiction but as a fact. Garnett combined the three functions of printer, business manager, and reporter. As the week went on he turned his own shorthand notes of meetings into type, cutting out altogether the intermediate process of translating shorthand into longhand, and when the paper was printed on Friday it was he who took off his jacket and turned the handle of the press. We must go back a little to introduce Jeremiah Garnett properly to the stage of public life in Manchester. He was the son of a certain William Garnett, a paper manufacturer of Otley, and was the youngest of three brothers who mastered many languages and sciences and rose by dint of this zeal for self-improvement to be men of mark, one of them in the Church, another in commerce at Clitheroe, and the third in journalism, the three together giving the family a name for learning and scholarship which was further improved in the generation which followed them by Dr. Richard Garnett, of the British Museum. Jeremiah was born in 1793, and, having been apprenticed to a printer at Barnsley, joined the service of *Wheeler's Manchester Chronicle* in 1814. John Edward Taylor invited him to assist in the establishment of the *Manchester Guardian*, with the standing of a junior partner. His ability as a practical printer was such that in 1828 he devised, with some expert assistance, a machine which raised the rate of printing the paper from 300 to 1500 copies in the hour. In later years his work was definitely literary and editorial, and it was indeed, as we shall see, under his editorship that the paper stood for some years rather by Palmerston than by Bright. His career furnishes a curious example of great determination, loyalty, and fervency in a strictly moderate position.

In the early career of Jeremiah Garnett we find some difficulty in separating his various functions as practical printer, business manager, and reporter. But it is nothing to the confusion which is caused by his having been at once a reporter and a public man. When Dr. Johnson was reporting the debates in Parliament there was always the opportunity to make the Whig dogs have the worst of it. It was a temptation, and Dr. Johnson succumbed to it. Garnett was under a more severe temptation still. He reported himself, and, even more to the point, he reported his antagonist. He was an extremely active man of affairs. In 1838 he and John Edward Taylor were added, in the distinguished company of Richard Cobden, to the Anti-Corn Law Association, when that body was but a week old. He was a member of the Manchester City Council. This was later. In the romantic morning of his career his main interests were in the parochial politics of the vestry and the street commissioners. In these dark and devious ways he knew every inch of the ground. He took a keen interest in the parish pump, which was indeed often stopped up. He was prominent at meetings of the " ley-payers," and excelled in the hostile and pessimistic examination of the churchwardens' accounts.

At these meetings Mr. Garnett is to be imagined fighting the battle of pure finance with sword and trowel, arraigning the church-warden and, at the close of his own fluent periods, seizing his pencil to take down the church-warden's reply. He can have known no rest. In the strain of this somewhat unnatural situation, his reports frequently passed beyond the sphere of mere record and became descriptive, com-mentatory, and highly partisan. He was fond of expressing a sort of *sotto voce* opinion within brackets. Thus, he interrupts his report of the speech of an opponent to make the reflection that while the orators of antiquity wrote their speeches Mr. —— goes one better and reads his from a printed copy, and reads it so fast that no one, and certainly not Jeremiah Garnett, can possibly take it down. Another member of the opposite party having alleged that the best point was left out of his speech in the *Guardian's* report of the last meeting, Mr. Garnett places the complaint on record, and appears again between his brackets, putting out his head to assure us that it shall not occur again. In future his readers will learn how " at this point Mr. —— sagaciously shook his head," or how " Mr. —— at this point drew from his fob his watch (gold, silver, or pinchbeck, as the case may be)

JOHN EDWARD TAYLOR,

Founder and first Editor of the *Manchester Guardian*. Born 1791 : died 1844.

and, looking at his watch with lack-lustre eye, said very wisely ' It is ten o'clock.' " He then becomes serious again, and, beginning with the words " Mr. Garnett said," gives a workman-like and, we should say, comprehensive summary of his own contribution to the debate. He stood up stoutly for the right of the press to be present at coroners' inquests, and carried a case on this point against the coroner to the King's Bench, when he lost, at an expense to the paper of £150. When the press finally secured the legal right of admittance he attended the first open sitting and had his revenge on the coroner in a footnote to his report.

§ II

The paper which issued in 1821 from the office at the corner of Market Street and New Cannon Street was thus rich in native ability, but not, at the moment, in anything else. It was laboriously printed by hand. The Stanhope press turned out at first only two hundred impressions of a single side in an hour, and twice that time was consequently needed to produce two hundred perfected copies. Its foreign news was all of it at least ten days old, and, though published on Saturday, it did not manage to bring its Parliamentary report beyond the preceding Wednesday night. Among its items of foreign news was a favourable account of the health of Napoleon Bonaparte, whose death had occurred before the words could be read. It was not until July that news of Napoleon's death reached the English press, the *Guardian* reporting it unofficially on July 7 and officially on July 14, when it added a list of the principal dates in his life, a predecessor of the modern obituary notice.

The first number contained forty-seven advertisements. One of them announces that a private house is to be let in Brazennose Street. Another one shows us that the present wide reputation of Ancoats has all been won in less than a hundred years. "Ancoats Hall," it says, "to let, together," it adds curtly, "with extensive gardens and pleasure grounds, stocked with choice fruit trees in full bearing." An advertisement is not always strictly true, but its inaccuracy is circumscribed by very definite limits, and we can but bow the head before this staggering assertion. A description of a "missing gentleman" has some historical value. It is evident that he was badly wanted, for the advertisement is repeated, but no one seems to have seen the figure in the "black coat and waistcoat, blue trousers, and Wellington boots, with a green silk umbrella," who thus flashes across the stage of life and makes his exit two miles from Manchester on the Cheetham Hill Road. Among the items of local news there is an agreeable account of the conduct of a colony of rooks which had lately established itself "in a garden at the top of King Street." Jackdaws, says Mr. Garnett, whose hand can be traced in this paragraph, were also present. The second number, issued on

May 12, contains the savage intelligence that Mary Slater (aged 33) has been sentenced at the Quarter Sessions to transportation for fourteen years for stealing a watch, a handkerchief, and twenty-six shillings. The " Births, Marriages, and Deaths " column began with the first number, but until the society of the town had been taught to use it—and perhaps to help in teaching them—it was largely compiled from the fashionable news of the London papers. The column announces, for example, the death, at Clifton, of Mrs. Piozzi, who as Mrs. Thrale figures conspicuously in Boswell's *Life of Johnson.*

The first public question we find agitated in the *Guardian* arose out of George IV's quarrel with his wife, which reached the height of scandal when the Queen was refused her crowning in Westminster Abbey, as she had already been shut out of the pages of the Prayer-book. The *Guardian* had all the Whig and Liberal sentiment for the Queen. It appeared in black for the first time for this same Caroline of Brunswick when she died a few days after the affair of the Coronation, and when the Government ordered her body to be taken round the suburbs of London on its way to Harwich for fear of trouble in the City, the *Guardian* published its first map, showing the circuitous and clandestine route.

Coronation Day in Manchester called forth the first strong interference of the *Guardian* in local affairs. A passage which is to be found in an issue of July 1821, announces that the social conscience—often called in later days the Nonconformist conscience—is awakening on a subject about which opinion had been fast asleep. The paper had been describing the procession round the town when the passage opens.

Here we should have been glad to close our account of the proceedings of the day, but we have a further duty to discharge—unpleasant and perhaps invidious. About five o'clock commenced the distribution of meat and beer to the populace. The stations for this were—the New Market, Shudehill; the Shambles at Bank Top; those at the top of Bridge Street; in Campfield Market; the George and Dragon, Ardwick; the Clarendon Public House, Chorlton Row; in Hulme, in Strangeways, in Motram's Field, and in Oldfield Road. At many, we fear we may say most, of these places scenes were exhibited which even the pencil of a Hogarth would fail to pourtray. At the New Market, Shudehill, the meat and loaves were thrown out high from the doors and windows of the warehouse where they had been stored; the populace scrambling for them as they could. It resembled the throwing of goods out of the windows of a warehouse on fire rather than anything else we can compare it to. There was shameful waste and general confusion. At an early hour the stage erected for the applicants to stand upon gave way, and one person was killed and several dangerously wounded by the fall.

When the liquor was distributing we saw whole pitchers thrown indiscriminately among the crowd—men holding up their hats to receive drink; people quarrelling and fighting for the possession of a jug;

the strong taking liquor from the weak ; boys and girls, men and women, in a condition of beastly drunkenness, staggering before the depository of ale or lying prostrate on the ground under every variety of circumstance and in every degree of exposure, swearing, groaning, vomiting, but calling for more liquor when they could not stand or even sit to drink it. Every kind of excess, indeed, which the most fertile imagination can conceive or the most graphic pen describe was there witnessed in nauseous and loathsome extravagance. Never did we see, and we hope to God never again shall see, human nature so degraded. The scenes of which we have now attempted a faint description were exhibited, though perhaps to scarcely the same extent, at Campfield, in Salford, and at the Shambles in Bridge Street ; and we trust the experience of this day will have given to the Committee who managed the proceedings a lesson which they will never forget. As to the distribution of meat and liquor, there are two or three lives lost and fourteen patients in the Infirmary, several of them dangerously injured, from the events of the day.

Two years before this incident Henry Hunt had been preaching total abstinence among his Radical followers. His motive was not so much evangelical as political. Total abstinence was one way of impoverishing a tyrannical Government, and Hunt tried, without success, to popularize a non-alcoholic beverage of his own invention. The agitation was checked by a leaflet in which drink and the drink habit were theologically extolled and sobriety stigmatized as a conspiracy against the King, the Church, and the Constitution. The production of this leaflet

53

and its distribution from door to door cost £80, which was defrayed from the church rates and included in the churchwardens' accounts, though an application to the King's Bench for further particulars of the item caused it eventually to be withdrawn. The scene in Manchester on the night of George IV's coronation, aided by the attention the *Guardian* called to it, set the temperance movement going in the town in real earnest.

The *Guardian* was exactly three years old when John Edward Taylor married his cousin, Sophia Russell Scott. Miss Scott was the daughter of the Rev. Russell Scott, who was for forty-five years the minister of the High Street (Unitarian) Chapel at Portsmouth. She was the devoted sister of a second Russell Scott, who rose to some eminence in the commerce of London and became the father of Mr. C. P. Scott, the present editor and proprietor of the *Manchester Guardian*. The attachment between John Edward Taylor and his cousin had begun before the *Guardian* was thought of, and their marriage was probably delayed until the venture should declare itself as between failure and success. In the following letter written by Miss Scott to her brother, Russell Scott, on May 8, 1821, we hear from her in her own words something which we already know about the foundation of the paper. We learn from it that John Edward Taylor did not contemplate abandoning at once and altogether his business in the cotton trade :

You are perhaps not aware that it has been for some time felt, both by Whigs and Reformers, that a well-conducted paper was much wanted in Manchester—one, to use Edward's words when he first wrote to me upon the subject, " which, from its character either as a spirited vehicle for the promulgation of their political opinions, or from the tone and style of its literary execution, would be considered worthy of the populous and intelligent district in which we are situated." " Cowdroy's " derived its chief value from the part Edward frequently took in it. Under these circumstances some of the most respectable and moderate persons in Manchester raised a subscription for the purpose of establishing a new newspaper, and they prevailed on Edward to become the editor. Their view was public advantage. They were willing to take the risk without wishing to have any share in the profits.

Edward's name does not appear, but it is generally known he is the editor, and indeed it was thought no one could establish a paper with equal prospects of success. It will not at all interfere with his business, as there is a person to take the labour of it ; besides which he writes and composes with greater facility than any person I ever saw. . . . I send you a prospectus by which you will see the first number was published on Saturday. Edward is very sanguine as to its success, indeed he has met with so much encouragement from all parties that it were impossible to be otherwise. It is indeed very gratifying to see how completely amidst all the party feeling which has existed he has won the confidence of all. This has been manifested in some very striking instances.

Writing again to her brother on March 7, 1823, Miss Scott throws some light on the early progress of the paper :

You will be glad to hear the *Guardian* continues to advance. Saturday week the edition was 1750. Of last week I have not heard, but there was a very good show of advertisements, and another puff extraordinary, stating that they could now venture to assert its sale exceeded any other Manchester paper, and consequently offered the best medium for advertisements.

Writing himself to Miss Scott on December 28, 1823, John Edward Taylor shows that this early progress is sustained and is even accelerating :

You would be astonished last week at the advertisements, wern't you, dear ? I was, at any rate. They kept pouring in so that I soon found there would be no room to spare for me, and therefore, as my men were forward with their work, I did what I have not done before on a Friday since I have had the *Guardian*, I went out to a 5 o'clock dinner, and stayed until 10 enjoying myself, and then returned to the office, and left it for home at $\frac{1}{2}$ past 2. The profit that week was upwards of £36, and there was so little room for news that I wrote off on the Friday night about a quantity of smaller type to enable me to compress the advertisements into less compass. This will be an expense of £150 or £170, which I did not intend incurring at present ; however, I really cannot say that I regret being obliged to do so.

I was looking a little last evening at the result of the half year, and I find the average of the advertisements for that time to be $73\frac{15}{26}$, and the average profit £21 6s. 7d. per week. If as I expect the profit on the newspaper and the job printing has been sufficient to pay all expenses, that will make the nett profit on the half year £550, and that is about what I expect to find. It will be a week or two, however,

before I am able to finish my stocktaking, and upon
that week or two I declare I almost look with dread.
. . . I think I told you I had promised to give my
friends a treat (an evening party) as soon as I had
passed the 100 advertisements, and this you see, my
dear, I have now done at a hand canter.

In the summer of 1825 John Edward Taylor
began the publication of a Tuesday's paper.
It was called the *Advertiser*. Within a few
weeks of its establishment Mr. Taylor became
the possessor by purchase of Harrop's *Mercury*,
which was also published on Tuesday. The two
papers were amalgamated under the name of
the *Manchester Mercury and Tuesday's General
Advertiser*, which continued to be published
until December, 1830. Mr. Taylor purchased
also from Mr. Harrop the *British Volunteer*.
This was incorporated with the *Guardian*, and
for a period of time the full title of the paper
was *The Manchester Guardian and British Volunteer*.

John Edward Taylor, writing on December
18, 1825, to Mr. Russell Scott, who had lent
important aid in these undertakings, says :

You will be glad to hear that hitherto the purchase
of Harrop's papers more than answers my expectations.
The sale the first Saturday [of *The Manchester Guardian
and British Volunteer*] was 3041, the second 3001, and
yesterday 3109. The most sanguine expectation I
took of the thing would have been satisfied with 2800.
The *Mercury* [the Tuesday paper], too, goes on well.
We have had on the average about 50 advertisements
each week, and are getting constantly some new sub-

scribers. Last week the sale was about 440. I do
not expect it ever to become very large.

§ III

On his marriage John Edward Taylor went
to live at No. 13, The Crescent, Salford. It
was one of the desirable quarters of the town.
A writer of about this period assures the inhabitants " of this charming elevation " that
they will " always be sure of rich rural scenery
in view of their front windows, however crowded
and confined the back part of their dwellings
may become. The fertile valley," he adds,
" the meandering of the river Irwell, approaching
to and receding from the Crescent, the rural cots,
the pleasant villas, the rising hills, and the distant
mountains never fail to create admiration as
often as the eye looks over the fascinating picture." The time was to come when The Crescent receded somewhat from these ripe perfections and Mr. Taylor's later days were spent at
Beech Hill, Cheetham Hill. Four children were
born of the marriage and three survived—Russell
Scott Taylor, the second editor of the *Guardian*,
whose promising career was cut short by an early
death ; Sophia Russell Taylor, who married Mr.
Peter Allen, and a second John Edward Taylor,
who was destined to carry on the *Guardian* for
many years. The spiritual home of the family
was the Cross Street Chapel, of which John
Edward Taylor remained an active and devoted
member to the day of his death. Until his

thirty-ninth year Mr. Taylor was physically a strong man. He lost the best of his health, as Huskisson, the statesman, afterwards lost his life, through the construction of the Liverpool and Manchester Railway. The railway itself was opened on September 15, 1830. In the autumn of 1829 engine trials were being held at Rainhill, and at one of these Mr. Taylor was present. The following letter, written by Mrs. John Edward Taylor on December 6, 1829, tells what occurred in terms which have a quaint ring :

I am sorry, my dear sister, you have been so uneasy about Edward ; he is, I am most thankful to tell you, now quite well. He had a series of colds one after the other till at last they ended in a serious illness, and before he got strong he went whisking through the air at an immense velocity on the Liverpool railroad without a greatcoat, which Mr. Whatton (the family doctor) called " a very young trick."

From this time forward Mr. Taylor suffered from a bronchial weakness which eventually, though not for many years yet, caused his death. Mrs. John Edward Taylor, in whose life and character Liberal Nonconformity had flowered into much beauty of mind and spirit, died in 1832. In 1836 Mr. Taylor married as his second wife Miss Harriet Acland Boyce, of Tiverton, by whom he had three children, one of whom married Stanley Jevons, the economist. Jeremiah Garnett produced his new machines in 1828, and the *Guardian* greatly improved on its personal appearance. For the first time the hand of the sub-editor began to appear. Hitherto, things, some of them useful and others merely curious, had got into its columns as they get into a schoolboy's pocket, by force,of gravitation and a profound unwillingness of the spirit to eject anything. But somebody was by now acquiring the courage of the blue pencil, and the things which were admitted were shown to their reserved seats and kept there. The markets begin to be grouped under a common heading. Law, politics, commerce, local news, and foreign news begin to find their settlements, and the paper shows its continuing enterprise by announcing on the eve of the Lancaster Assizes that a reporter will, as usual, attend.

By this time the local ground had been cleared of a dense and stunted eighteenth-century journalism. There were fewer papers and those which were left standing were shooting up. The triumvirate of *Guardian*, *Courier*, and *Examiner* was all of it now in being. In 1824, Mr. Archibald Prentice, minor prophet and historian of the Manchester School, bought the remnants of *Cowdroy's Gazette* from the widow of William Cowdroy and transformed it into the *Manchester Gazette*. In 1827 it failed, but was revived the next year for Mr. Prentice's benefit as the *Manchester Gazette and Times*, and developed in 1848 into the *Manchester Examiner and Times*, illustrious for the long editorship of Mr. Henry Dunckley. The *Courier* was a year younger than the *Examiner*. Mr. Thomas Sowler, who founded it, was a bookseller, and our first tidings of him are obtained from an announcement in the *Guardian* that he is willing to receive advertisements and other communications for the paper at his shop in St. Ann's Square. He was thus brought into relationship with journalism, and when the Tory and Anti-Catholic party in Manchester began to find themselves, as they now did, dangerously outdone in the press, Mr. Sowler came to their help with the *Courier*, which appeared on January 1, 1825. The proprietor and his advisers made an ambitious choice of an editor for the new paper. The call for reform and the call for Catholic relief were swelling considerably ; the laws which penalized Dissent were all but gone. These Liberal causes had many friends now even in the House of Lords. Earl Grey, cold and silvery but still a planet, was rising in the skies. Earl Fitzwilliam had been dismissed from the Lord Lieutenancy of the West Riding for Liberal sympathies. On the Tory side, these were no times for the Wheelers and Harrops and other men of unlimited prejudices but few words. Mr. Alaric Watts was accordingly chosen to be editor of the *Courier*, in the hope that a professional writer and the personal friend of Scott and Wordsworth and Coleridge would be more than a match for the native literary talent of the Taylors and Garnetts and Prentices.

The Whig *Guardian* and the Tory *Courier*

61

began a private and personal feud which lasted till the turn of journalistic manners, after which they fell under a kind of anæsthesia as to one another's existence, the one never mentioning the other by name again. In the days when speaking terms still subsisted, the speaking and the being spoken to were, on the side of the *Guardian*, done chiefly by Mr. Garnett. We find Mr. Garnett characterized in the *Courier* as " an impudent and wilful perverter of the truth," as " a blockhead," and as " a defender of national infidelity." Mr. Garnett is found accusing the *Courier* alliteratively of a " crawling and cowardly lie." The feeling between Mr. Garnett and Mr. Sowler ran very high. They all but fought a duel. Mr. Garnett, though called upon by Mr. Sowler's " second," declined the duel with pistols, but evinced no objection an hour or two later to a meeting with umbrellas in St. Ann's Square, whence the matter was removed and adjourned to the police court. This incident occurred on July 24, 1839.

Long before this the *Guardian* had definitely settled down to a middle position in politics. It was a Whig paper, and cautious even at that. These were days when great cities and large houses remained voteless and voiceless in the House of Commons ; in which Roman Catholics were helots and Nonconformists only just tolerated. A savage Corn Law, passed in the interests of rent, barred at once the entrance of foreign food and the exit of English manufactures, to the great bewilderment of politicians who wished it to serve the one end and not the other. These were grievances which affected the middle-class. The working-class shared them, and had many which were peculiar to itself. Through it all the *Guardian* remained studiously moderate and opportunistic. It was extraordinarily unspeculative. "We are not," said Cicero, "in the republic of Plato, but in the mud of Romulus." In the spirit of this admonition the *Guardian* wanted the next thing next. The next thing was to reform a system of representation which allowed one hundred boroughs whose united population did not equal that of Manchester and Salford to send two hundred members to Parliament, while Manchester and Salford were without one.

At the beginning of 1828 John Edward Taylor was drawn, and perhaps driven, by his Radical critics into a more compendious confession of faith. He pronounced himself in favour of the removal of civil disabilities for religious beliefs, the improvement and ultimate removal of the Corn Laws, severe economy in public departments, the amendment of the game laws, and the abolition of various trading monopolies with the West Indies, India, and China. Banking and currency reform greatly interested him. He thought the distinction between Whig and Tory might go, as indeed it soon did, and that a new division might be made between "Political Economists" and "Monopolists." This also occurred, though the names of " Liberal " and " Conservative," which were chosen to express much the same idea, were perhaps a more convenient currency. So much for his positives. His negatives were not few. We suspect that he did not wish too popular a franchise. We know that he was against shorter Parliaments and the ballot, and on the question of the Corn Laws he had not yet learned to pronounce the magic name " repeal." " A fixed duty is a fixed injustice " were the words on the scroll which ran in one piece round the Free Trade Hall in the early forties. John Edward Taylor was not yet quite of this mind.

But he was becoming every year a much more versatile and resourceful editor. He was collecting a staff. In 1830 he made a journey to Hull to secure a particularly promising reporter. This was a certain John Harland, who had been trained as a printer but had made himself the most expert shorthand writer in the country. John Harland was brought to Manchester and served the *Guardian* as its chief reporter for thirty years. His importance in the history of journalism and his eminence as a Lancashire antiquary have caused his useful life to be commemorated in the *Dictionary of National Biography*. No fewer than three members of the *Guardian* connection of this time—Taylor, Garnett, and Harland—were destined to figure honourably in that great gallery of English notability.

IV : CLASSICAL MANCHESTER

CHAPTER IV

Classical Manchester

§ I

IT is with strong emotions of joy and hope, says the leading article in the *Manchester Guardian* of June 9, 1832, that we announce the fact that the English Reform Bill has at length become the law of the land. Now that the Reform Bill has passed, the editor proceeded, it is proper that the electors of Manchester should apply themselves seriously to the important question, who are to be their representatives. . . . There is not one of the new boroughs—probably there is not one place, borough or county, invested with the elective franchise, the proceedings in which at the ensuing election will be watched with such intense anxiety as those of Manchester. It depends on the constituency of this town to give a practical proof of the validity of their claim to be invested with the franchise by the discreet and conscientious mode in which they exercise it. The representatives of Manchester, the metropolis of the most important trade of the kingdom, ought to be able to exert not a mere personal but a high degree of moral influence in the House of Commons. They should be men of mature age, sound judgment, good talents improved by sedulous cultivation, irreproachable private character, and thoroughly liberal public principles. Wealth is no absolutely indispensable requisite ; yet undoubtedly they ought to have at least the means of maintaining with independence and without serious personal sacrifice the unavoidable expenses attendant on their station.

With this grave benediction the electoral history of Manchester began. We are under no illusions at this time of day about the Reform Act of 1832. For every person whom it satisfied it disappointed at least ten. The population of Manchester was 181,768. The number of voters on the new register was only 4293, and it may be calculated that at least six families in seven were left unrepresented. It is a curious fact that the unrepresented did not immediately perceive what had happened to them. Two months after the bill passed the town rose *en masse* and welcomed it with a public holiday, which passed off very well considering that so many people must have been prone to two reflections, the one that they had not themselves personally been endowed with any share in the British Constitution, and the second that they might on the other hand be participating at any minute in the Asiatic cholera which was raging through the town. The *Guardian* describes the proceedings at great length, and the report gives us an interesting exhibition of a Bank Holiday in its infancy.

The procession was formed at ten o'clock in the morning at The Crescent in Salford, and marched by way of Chapel Street, Blackfriars Street, St. Mary's Gate, Market Street, and High Street, where it followed a route no longer processional to Ardwick Green, which was then a much-favoured spot, and had only recently been described by a local author as the most desirable suburb in England. On Ardwick Green there was a pond, and from a bridge thrown

68

across this pond—the gentry occupying the most favoured stations around the edge of the water, the others in less advantageous positions, though still commanding a full view, and every pair of eyes in the town directed expectantly up—Mr. Charles Green, the celebrated aeronaut, proceeded to release a balloon cunningly shaped and painted to represent Earl Grey, and when the extreme diversion which this object continued to cause as long as it remained in sight was at an end he proceeded, amid breathless attention, to make an ascent himself. In order to bring home to the mind of the people how completely he had cut himself off from his mother earth, Mr. Green, when at an altitude of three thousand feet, as the *Guardian* reporter computed it, released a goose from the car, which, " after falling a few yards, recovered the use of its wings, took an angle of 60 to 70 degrees, and appeared to alight in safety." When he was much higher still Mr. Green liberated a parachute, the basket of which contained a cat. The parachute descended in a field near to Newton, and the cat was restored in safety to " No. 3 gasworks," where it ordinarily lived.

Mr. Green had by this time vanished, but it was rumoured truthfully in the town in the evening that he also had come to earth near Rochdale. Meanwhile the procession had been re-formed and had finally disbanded itself in St. Ann's Square. The watchmen of the town had figured very conspicuously in the day's pageantry. They marched at the end of the procession, 130 in number, and wearing their watchmen's coats and gold-laced hats. The watchmen also carried their sticks and rattles, and at intervals during the progress of the procession the *Guardian* tells us that they " sprang their rattles," sometimes in divisions and sometimes all together, but never failing to produce a very singular noise.

Meanwhile the *Guardian* had been holding a weekly review of the possible Parliamentary candidates. The choice of candidates was not managed without a definite and public split between the Whigs and those who were now beginning to call themselves Radicals. On one candidate Whigs and Radicals were agreed. It was to be Mark Philips. Mark Philips, to whom belongs the title of " first member for Manchester," or more exactly " first senior member for Manchester," was the son of Mr. Robert Philips, a partner in the firm of J. and N. Philips and Co., of Church Street. He was born in 1800, and made his entrance into public life in Manchester in 1826 at a reformers' meeting in the Manor Court-room, at which, being in his way rather a " catch," he was received with open arms, and paid for his welcome with a very promising speech against the Corn Laws. He continued to be the member for Manchester until 1847, taking a distinguished part in the Free Trade campaign on the floor of the House of Commons and on the platform of the Free Trade Hall. When the battle was won he retired

to a country life in Warwickshire, but remained
a faithful member of the Liberal party, making
his last appearance in Manchester in October,
1871, at the banquet which celebrated the opening of the Reform Club in that year. His name
is commemorated in Philips Park. In his address
to the electors in 1832 Mark Philips pronounced
for shorter Parliaments, the ballot, public economy, the removal of the taxes on knowledge,
the repeal of the Corn Laws ("the greatest and
most oppressive of all monopolies"), the reform
of the existing system of supporting the Church,
and the abolition of tithes. The *Guardian*,
though "not able to go with Mr. Philips in all
his views," accepted him cordially as the first
candidate of the Whig party.

For the second candidate the choice of the
Guardian fell on Mr. S. J. Loyd, a banker of
great wealth and eminence, who had descended
on the constituency from the City of London,
though he was not without a business connection
with Manchester. Loyd was a friend of Senior,
the economist, and Grote, the historian, and his
standing in the City of London was such that
when, in a later chapter of history, he became
definitely converted though rather late in the
day to Free Trade and sent a subscription to the
League it was generally felt in all the clubs that
the Corn Laws were past praying for. He was
much the same kind of politician as those whom
we knew at a recent election as "Unionist Free-
traders," and had the high moral authority,

71

not to say sanctity, of that connection. John Edward Taylor attended the first of his meetings in Manchester, and put to him the question of questions—whether, had he been in Parliament, he would have supported the Reform Bill. The answer was not given without some circumlocution. But Mr. Taylor was satisfied, and from that time forward his candidates were Philips and Loyd. Unhappily the Radicals would not accept Loyd, and at the end of several weeks, in which their proceedings were watched with great anxiety, they produced from their sleeve Mr. Charles Poulett Thomson, Vice-President of the Board of Trade in Lord Grey's Administration, a budding Free-trader, and so good a friend to the rights of man that Jeremy Bentham had personally canvassed for him in Dover.

There is no doubt that the *Guardian* would have liked to support Poulett Thomson, but it held by its pledge to Loyd at the cost of nearly all its enjoyment of the contest. The Tories put up Mr. J. T. Hope, who, having no earthly prospect of success and being a very delightful and aristocratic young man, became the spoiled darling of the contest, and was indulged in everything short of actual votes. New Cross had a candidate almost entirely to itself in William Cobbett. The *Guardian* never could away with William Cobbett, and its long reports of his speeches are often to be found prefaced with the somewhat curt introduction, "This person said."

More specifically, it described him as "an unprincipled demagogue and consummate quack," and indeed the main ground of the *Guardian's* objection to Poulett Thomson was lest three Reform candidates should "let in" the unspeakable Cobbett.

On the morning of December 12 the town knew by the early ringing of the Collegiate Church bells that the election day had arrived. The modern reader is to imagine the hustings erected in St. Ann's Square, close to the palisading of the church and facing the spot where the statue of Cobden now stands. Six boxes of the shape associated with the Punch and Judy show formed the hustings. The Boroughreeve, with the churchwardens, the sidesmen, and the reporters, occupied the central box, and each of the other compartments held a candidate with a select body of his supporters, the whole company presenting to the crowd below a complete selection of current political opinion and a very striking array of blue, claret, and bottle-green broadcloth, stovepipe hats, high stocks, side whiskers, and ingratiating expressions of face. On the ground immediately below stood five hundred special constables, and behind the special constables the firemen.

The beadle rang his bell and proclaimed silence ; the Boroughreeve took the oath, and the long process of nominating and seconding each candidate began. It was a fatal obstacle to the smooth working of this part of the proceedings that each nominator and seconder was a local man known intimately and in all his most vulnerable points to the wit and mischief of the town. The first speaker had not proceeded for more than a moment or two, and the early novelty of seeing a familiar face in unfamiliar surroundings had hardly worn away, when someone in the crowd recovered his self-possession and directed a telling shaft at the personal appearance or the domestic circumstances of the speaker, some debt for which he had sued or been sued, his tendency to be too thrifty or not thrifty enough, or any other intimate personal particular which, though it had nothing to do with the argument in hand, was calculated to import into it much ridicule or prejudice. The friends of the speaker were much mortified by this palpable hit, and from this time forward the gentlemen in the hustings gazed down over their stocks at a scene of irrecovered and irrecoverable pandemonium. At the first election the beadle rang his bell almost incessantly from a quarter past nine in the morning till a quarter past one, when the Boroughreeve was understood though not heard to be proclaiming Philips and Cobbett elected on a show of hands. A poll was demanded in dumb show by all the other candidates, and this took place on the two following days, with the result that the two Reform candidates, Philips and Poulett Thomson, were elected by a comfortable majority, the *Guardian* accepting the result with pleasure tempered with a mild regret for the defeat of Mr. Loyd, who had not been quite sound and satisfactory on the question of the slave trade. The country had to wait many years yet for the ballot, and it throws a curious light on the system of open voting to find the *Guardian* severely censuring a barrister and a merchant whom its reporter had caught in the act of voting for Cobbett. The election was treated to seven and a half columns of the *Guardian's* narrow space.

In the same number a lady in Ancoats advertises for a footman of undoubted respectability, and elegant apartments are offered to a gentleman in a small family in the neighbourhood of the Portico in Mosley Street. It was not impossible about this time to find " a drawing-room and one or two bedrooms to be let in Piccadilly," and, a year or two later than 1832, a young man who resided in the country announced himself in the *Guardian* as " desirous of dining with a respectable family daily at one o'clock within five minutes' walk of the Exchange." But the town was on the eve of great changes. It was in 1832 that Mr. Brooks, of the firm of Cunliffe and Brooks, the bankers, broke in on the residential gentility of Mosley Street by converting his house in that street into a warehouse. Richard Cobden soon afterwards did the same thing, moving his residency for another twelve years into Quay Street. With the fall of residential Mosley Street we begin to hear of the rise of Rusholme and Broughton and Pendleton. The Victorian

75

detached house, with its carriage drive and its stables and banks of rhododendra, begins to take the place of the eighteenth-century town house which disdained not to stand in a row and open on to a street. And when the change came, it came so rapidly and spared so little that eighteenth-century Manchester is now almost as difficult to find as mediæval Manchester. There is still a conspicuous Tudor fragment in Market Place. As for the eighteenth century, it has to be reconstructed from an occasional domestic door-way—perhaps the remnants of a torch extinguisher—to a warehouse, though there is a sustained similitude of it in St. John Street. In this street, though frightened not a little by the doctors' automobiles, the eighteenth century still lingers. It may be traced in the architecture of the street ; still more in the interiors of the houses, in their shutter-boxes, and in the sweeping curves of their staircases.

An early sign of the new age which was opening now that a reformed Parliament had met was the removal of some of the duties on newspapers. In 1833 the duty on advertisements was reduced from three-and-sixpence to one-and-sixpence, and in 1836 the price of the stamp was lowered from fourpence to one penny. The *Guardian* responded to this better weather by lowering its price in the autumn of 1836 to fourpence and by appearing twice a week, adding a Wednesday's issue to the older issue of Saturday. The market report in the

Wednesday edition proved extremely useful to business men, and the hold of the paper on commercial Manchester was strengthened by it not a little.

§ II

The week beginning on December 13, 1838, was an eventful one in the life of Richard Cobden. On that day there was a meeting of the Manchester Chamber of Commerce. The directors had drafted a meek and mild petition to Parliament on the subject of the Corn Laws, and they now asked the members of the Chamber to sanction it. The members were about to do so when Mr. Cobden rose from a remote corner of the room and attacked the Corn Laws in a speech of such argument and conviction that it completely changed the temper of the meeting. The directors were obliged to take back their petition and to consent to an adjournment of the meeting for a week. On the next day another cause in which Mr. Cobden was deeply concerned was, not advanced but finally won. The first municipal council for Manchester was elected, and Mr. Cobden was returned as a councillor for St. Michael's Ward. John Edward Taylor, who had also laboured long and hard for incorporation, was elected for St. Ann's Ward. Among the other new councillors were Henry Tootal, Elkanah Armitage, William Romaine Callender, S. D. Darbishire, and Thomas Potter. The first meeting of the Council was held on the next day, when Mr. Cobden was made an alderman and proposed Joseph Heron for the office of Town Clerk. Three days of the week were thus busily occupied, and on the seventh day the Chamber of Commerce met again, and Mr. Alderman Cobden carried his resolution in favour of total repeal and became thereby the marked man of the agitation which was now beginning in earnest and was to make Manchester for eight years the political centre and capital of England.

Two years before this an Anti-Corn Law Association had been formed in London with several distinguished politicians and literary men in its membership, but the climate was against it, and it did not flourish. The City of London finally came into the movement, but not for several years yet. There had been a sporadic outbreak of the agitation in Bolton, where a young medical student, Mr. A. W. Paulton, who was to become later on a distinguished spokesman of the League, had been lecturing brilliantly on Free Trade. But the historic starting point of the affair was a little meeting called by Archibald Prentice and addressed by Dr. Bowring, the traveller and economist, in the York Hotel in Manchester on September 10, 1838. Out of this meeting grew the Manchester Anti-Corn Law Association, which was in its turn the nucleus of the Anti-Corn Law League. John Bright was an original member. Richard Cobden joined when the Association was

1 R. Cobden.
2 Wm. Rawson.
3 John Bright.
4 C. P. Villiers.
5 T. M. Gibson.
6 Geo. Wilson.
7 R. H. Greg.
8 John Brooks.
9 J. B. Smith.
10 Earl Ducie.
11 Earl Radnor
12 Archibd. Prentice.
13 Col. Thompson.
14 Wm. Brown (Liverpool).

15 Hamer Stansfeld.
16 Thos Bazley.
17 Hy. Ashworth.
18 Jas Chadwick.
19 Wm. Bickham.
20 Hy Rawson.
21 Saml. Lees.
22 Thos Woolley.
23 Wm. Evans.
24 Jas. Lumsden.
25 Jos. Hickin (Secretary).
26 Lord Kinnaird
27 Rev. Dr. Massie.
28 John Whittaker.

29 Robt. Ashton
30 Duncan McLaren.
31 Jas. Wilson (London).
32 A. W. Paulton.
33 Wm. Biggs.
34 John Petrie.
35 C. E. Rawlins junr
36 Jas Garth Marshall.
37 Robert Mann.
38 John Dixon (Carlisle).
39 Jos. Schofield.
40 Fredk. Schwann.
41 Lawrence Heyworth.
42 Robt Gilligan.

43 W. J. Fox.
44 Francis Place.
45 Edwd. Baines.
46 Edwd. Baxter (Dundee).
47 P. A. Taylor.
48 Dr. Bowring.
49 John Cheetham.
50 Jos. Brotherton.
51 Saml. Bean.
52 Jas. Kershaw.
53 W. R. Callender.
54 Sir Thos Potter.
55 Thos. Ashton.

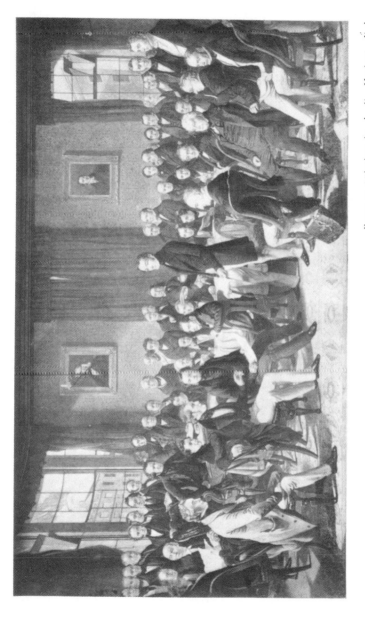

From a painting by J. R. Herbert, R.A.

MR. COBDEN ADDRESSING THE COUNCIL OF THE ANTI CORN LAW LEAGUE.

By permission of Messrs. T. Agnew & Sons.

about a week old, and with him joined John Edward Taylor and Jeremiah Garnett, of the *Manchester Guardian*. In the lists of its earliest members and subscribers occur the names of Armitage, Ashton, Bannerman, Greg, Philips, Rylands, and Watts.

We cannot here follow all the movements of an organization which developed such resources of money and enthusiasm and ability as to become in truth another estate of the realm. The conventions which began from this time forward to be held in Manchester were not only orgies of eloquence but parliaments of manufacturing and Dissenting England. Manchester was Mecca. By 1840 it had been found that the town had no meeting place anything like large enough to hold the streams of pilgrims, and at the beginning of that year there was erected on the site of the present Free Trade Hall a wooden pavilion which was by far the largest place of public assembly in the country. The land on which this pavilion stood was lent to the Association by Mr. Cobden, to whom it belonged. In 1843 the pavilion was taken down, and the first Free Trade Hall, the predecessor of the present building, erected in its place. The opening of this hall was the first event in a great week of convention. The volume of the speaking which was done in Manchester that week may be estimated from the fact that the report in the *Manchester Guardian* of Wednesday measures no fewer than thirty-nine close columns of print out of a possible forty-eight, and the meetings were still continuing when the paper went to press.

Both the Pavilion of 1840 and the Free Trade Hall of 1843 were opened with banquets. But the League did not habitually dine. It belonged to the middle-class, and it took tea. Its characteristic function was the tea-party. The League held tea-parties everywhere. Mammoth tea-parties were held in the Free Trade Hall and the Corn Exchange in Manchester, and the ministers' vestries and deacons' vestries of a widespread Nonconformity emptied themselves into these gatherings without experiencing any change of atmosphere. The League all but invented the bazaar. Its bazaars in the Theatre Royal in Manchester and Covent Garden Theatre in London stand alongside the Art Treasures Exhibitions of the time, and were not outdone by them. These tea-parties and bazaars were the cause of the first appearance of women in active public life in England. Ladies " presided at " tea-tables and served at stalls. The *Guardian* gives their names in long lists, and Bastiat, the French economist, who was watching things on the spot, told the French people of this as of something new and strange. Subscriptions to the £50,000, the £60,000, and the £250,000 Funds were announced and often thrown on the table in the Free Trade Hall amid scenes of ecstasy. The League drew upon vast resources of platform ability which was second only to that of

Cobden and Bright and Fox, and the *Guardian* of the time gives us the impression that everyone of importance in the town could make a speech like Peel. George Wilson, who presided over all the great meetings, is said to have developed such a virtuosity of chairmanship that no one has equalled him in that capacity before or since.

On the eve of Peel's surrender, in 1846, the last of all these great meetings was held in the Free Trade Hall. Even in the plain and almost hackneyed language of the *Guardian* reporter we can feel the height which feeling had reached. " Before seven o'clock," he says, " platform, galleries, and floor were crammed to a degree we never before witnessed. About twenty-five past seven Mr. George Wilson took the chair. He was accompanied by R. Cobden, Esq., J. Bright, Esq., W. J. Fox, Esq., and Colonel Thompson. The cheering from all parts of the hall as these gentlemen were recognized was tremendous." The reporter renders the deepest homage in his power to William Johnson Fox by reporting him, and him alone, in the first person. Here are his concluding words :

It is here, it is coming, the end of this struggle, and, come when it will, the testimony shall be borne not only here but all over the country that you, the men of Manchester, you have done it. All else has been subsidiary. Philosophers have laid down the principles. Statisticians have collected the facts and arranged the results. Politicians are but the machinery by which these results are to be reduced to legislative

81

practice. Queen, Lords, and Commons will be but the formal agents to give solemn record and authority to that which, whenever and however accomplished, originated in Manchester, originated with you. (Great cheering as the speaker resumed his seat, after a speech of about an hour's duration.)

The *Manchester Guardian* never compromised on the full doctrine of Free Trade. But it was not the organ of the Anti-Corn Law League. The Anti-Corn Law League did much with which it could not agree, and it was on the whole rather frightened of this tremendous neighbour in Newall's Buildings. There were three ways to the Free Trade conversion of 1846. There was Sir Robert Peel's way—his way was a more or less sudden conversion—and there was the way of the League, which for eight years demanded total and immediate repeal, and would not hear of anything short of this. Between the resistant Peel on the one hand and the insistent League on the other stood the Whig party, which underwent a gradual conversion and was in favour of instalments of reform. The *Guardian* wanted full Free Trade, and never ceased to preach full Free Trade, but it was always willing to accept a small fixed duty in exchange for the hated sliding scale, this small fixed duty to be improved away altogether as time and opportunity served. In 1841 the League intruded upon a by-election at Walsall, drove a Whig candidate out of the field because he could not pledge himself to total repeal, and committed what was to John Edward Taylor the unpardonable offence of " letting a Tory in."

The comments of the *Guardian* on this occurrence speak what was in this age its permanent mind about the doctrinaire spirit in politics :

Most of our readers are aware that the town is blessed by the presence and the labours of a number of gentlemen who call themselves philosophical reformers, and who profess to regulate all their political conduct by a strict adherence to certain dogmas which they call principles, without paying the slightest regard to expediency or accepting the slightest compromise with persons of different opinions. Now, all this sounds very fine in theory, but when reduced to practice, whether in politics or the ordinary business of life, it is not found to be a remarkably successful course of proceeding. It is undoubtedly true that the nearest route from one place to another is by a straight line, but if a coachman who regulated his conduct by this principle and scorned expediency were to endeavour to drive in a straight line from Manchester to London, his plan would end very much like most of the schemes of our political reformers ; he would either upset the coach or stick fast in a ditch before he had completed half a mile of his journey.

Here is another example of Taylor's teaching. It is taken from the *Guardian* of January 29, 1840:

We hold that all protecting duties, whether imposed on agricultural produce or on manufactured commodities, are either elusive or pernicious—that when they have any effect at all it is that of directing capital and labour into channels which are comparatively unprofitable. We therefore disapprove of any duty upon the import of corn, either fixed or fluctuating, as being erroneous in principle and injurious to the interests of the people. At the same time we are not amongst those who call out for a total repeal or nothing. We cannot conceal from ourselves that there are interests and prejudices to be encountered to which some respect must be paid ; and therefore as a preliminary step to that perfectly free trade which we believe to be both desirable and necessary for the country we would not object to the establishment *pro tempore* of a really moderate fixed duty.

§ III

Within the limits he thus defined for himself John Edward Taylor was always true to the Manchester policy. He did not, however, live to see it prevail, for his death occurred, at the age of 53, early in 1844. It would be idle to deny that his management of the *Manchester Guardian* had disappointed the Radical party of Manchester. John Edward Taylor lived and died a faithful Whig. Unfortunately his life as an editor lies on and overlies the sharp summit of Whig history. He had stumbled and struggled with Russell and Grey on the hard and dangerous road to the repeal of the Test and Corporation Act and the Reform Bill, and he lived to wander round and round with Melbourne in a singularly unrefreshing and miasmic valley of politics. When he finally laid down his practised pen the hope of the future was not with the Whigs at all, but with a new Liberal party, taking its inspiration from Peel, and through Peel from the young William Pitt, who had been the pupil of Adam Smith.

In journalism, as well as in politics, he lived at the fag-end of an epoch. In the very year of his death the first telegraph lines were laid, and within four years the *Guardian* was beginning to contain sparse fragments of news which had come " by electric telegraph." This event re-made his profession. Other events were breaking up the compact society in which he had lived. We might date a decisive modern Manchester from about 1840 to 1845, in which period Cobden risked and lost a competency by colonising Victoria Park. Or we might say that it was definitely established in the early fifties, when the omnibuses were splashing heavily every hour into the provincial peace of Pendleton and Broughton, and Central Manchester had begun to exhibit by night the trance-like condition of a seaside pool left by the receded tide of population and sparsely inhabited by the abstruse life of policemen and caretakers and cats.

If these changes had taken place in the shape of society there were still more definite changes in its speed. The Whitsuntide of 1846 was notable for its great increase in railway excursions, for periods varying from one to ten days. It was estimated that in five days of that festival nearly 16,000 people had travelled from Manchester to Liverpool. New Brighton was beginning to be very highly thought of at once for its air and its amenities, and it was for the next twenty years a favourite resort of the newly married. We begin to hear for the first time, in 1846, of Lytham and Blackpool.

The opening of the second Free Trade Hall in 1843 had been the occasion of a curious outbreak of modernity. The hall was opened with a banquet, and, when the tables for the banquet were spread, hundreds of people were admitted into the galleries to feast vicariously on the spectacle of so many knives and forks. The silver was afterwards sold by auction, the chairman's carving-knife fetching £3 4s. as an historical curiosity. After the banquet the League threw the hall open to the public for a few nights, charging them a small sum to come in. Davies's Manchester Band was put on the platform, and innocuous refreshments were to be had. The town exhibited a new-born taste for simple pleasures. It responded by " promenading," and even had the self-management to improve the promenade into a dance. The *Guardian* sent its reporter every night and watched over the proceedings with great benevolence.

Last evening we visited the hall, and were much gratified at the lively scene before us. Numerous groups were promenading on the floor ; others were seated taking lemonade or coffee. Davies's really good band, stationed on the dais, was playing lively airs ; the place was agreeably warm, and the scene was of the most pleasing and animated character. In a while the band commenced playing a favourite set of quadrilles ; three sets of dancers were formed as if by magic. We were much pleased to observe the decorum and propriety and the ease with which the dancers of both sexes went through the evolution of the figure. .... Had we such spacious halls permanently in our large commercial and manufacturing towns and so dedicated to innocent pleasures there can be no doubt that their citizens would soon acquire a taste for simple social fêtes equal to that which characterises our Continental neighbours.

John Edward Taylor was succeeded in the editorship by his eldest son. This son, Russell Scott Taylor, was of such advanced and even premature capacity that he was thought to be able to take his father's place at the early age of eighteen years. Oxford and Cambridge were not at that time open to one of so pronounced a Nonconformity, but, even so, the cause of higher education was not desperate. Especially was it not desperate in Manchester. Hardly even by searching can we find the end of the personal riches of Manchester in the day when Russell Scott Taylor was a maturing boy in his father's house at Cheetham Hill. In 1840 Manchester New College returned from York to its birth-place in Manchester, and it is an impressive fact, and one which might well cause us to reconsider our latter state, that while Manchester was re-shaping the politics of England such men as James Martineau, Francis William Newman, and William Gaskell were included in its academic citizenship, Martineau teaching philosophy and political economy, Newman Latin and Gaskell English history and literature in a sectarian academy in Grosvenor Square.

This rich professorate was attended by Russell Scott Taylor. It was also attended by his younger brother, the second John Edward Taylor, who was destined to a much larger and more enduring place in the history of the *Guardian*. For the brilliant promise of Russell Scott Taylor's life was not allowed to ripen into a corresponding performance. He died of typhoid fever in 1848 in the twenty-fourth year of his age, and about a year after his marriage with Miss Emily Acland. To his ability for public life he had joined much amiability and earnestness of private character, and during his editorship of the *Guardian* he continued to be an assiduous teacher in the Lower Mosley Street Sunday School. The younger John Edward Taylor, who had been born in 1830 and was now only eighteen years old, was too young to be the immediate successor of his very exceptional brother. From Manchester New College he passed on to the University of Bonn. On his return from Germany he was called to the Bar at the Inner Temple, but he returned to Manchester in time to take a large share in the newspaper developments which we shall find occurring about the middle fifties, and to begin his long term of office first in the immediate and afterwards in the ultimate headship of the *Manchester Guardian*.

V : *WHIGGISM*

CHAPTER V

Whiggism

§ I

FROM 1848 until 1861 the *Manchester Guardian* was edited by Jeremiah Garnett, the junior partner of its first proprietor. We left Garnett some years behind us in our narrative, the *enfant terrible* of journalism in Manchester, a satirist and one who dipped his pen in acid, somewhat of a swashbuckler and, but for the grace of God, a duellist. We saw him join the Manchester Anti-Corn Law Association in the momentous company of Cobden. He had been powerfully at the back of the incorporation of Manchester, and when John Edward Taylor died he took the vacant seat on the City Council. He was now at the age of fifty-five, in the middle years of life, which were to carry him slowly and insensibly to an old age of much moral and physical beauty.

On the political side, however, something untoward had happened to him at a date which we cannot precisely determine. The same thing had happened to many illustrious and invaluable Whigs, and was much commented upon by contemporary Radicals, who called them cases of "finality," having their origin in overstrain incurred at some period or other during the struggle for Reform and not noticed at the time, but causing now a kind of lethargy accompanied by a marked twisting of the neck backwards.

One may read of its effects in the life of Lord John Russell. Garnett had it. Garnett was, moreover, a water-tight Free-trader. Free Trade with him did not spill over into international sentiment. Writing to Cobden in 1857, Bright makes some comments on the length to which he and his friend had drawn ahead of the public opinion of their time. They had totally changed the creed and the policy of England on all questions relating to commerce, Customs duties, and taxation. They had established the notion of colonial self-government, and had persuaded all parties of the need for a wider measure of Parliamentary reform. So far Bright was able to congratulate the Manchester School on things definitely done. He was on more doubtful ground when he claimed that the " School " had also effected a revolution on questions relating to the Church. No one nowadays rends his garments as Bright habitually rent his at the mere phenomenon and spectacle of a bishop in the House of Lords or even in a 'bus. In the region of international co-operation and good-will he admitted that the " School " had so far failed. In this he was right, and it is a curious historical fact that the age of the fifties, which watched Gladstone by his successive Budgets completing the work of Peel and carrying the Free Trade principle into every cellar and passage of our fiscal system, should also have been contemporaneously the period of some of the highest handling and the highest prancing

JEREMIAH GARNETT

First printer, business manager and reporter of the *Manchester Guardian,* and from 1848 till 1861 its Editor.

our foreign policy has ever known. It was the age of Palmerston and Palmerston's *civis Romanus*. Garnett was of the school of Palmerston, and he made the *Guardian* an organ of the Palmerstonian Liberalism. He did not mean by Free Trade the larger millennial things which Cobden meant, and, though the *Guardian* by leading articles and by reports, and still more by its great influence over moderate opinion in Lancashire had done the League incalculable service, both John Edward Taylor and Garnett, and Garnett perhaps more particularly, had been rather with the movement than of it. Ten years after the victory of 1846 we find Garnett excessively irritated by the ghost of the League. It still walked. There is a passage in a letter by Cobden, of 1857, which indicates that the League was still an embodied thing, and Cobden seems to suggest that this was against his better judgment. It had been heard to boast that it still kept the key to the representation of Manchester at its home in Newall's Buildings. Its older local members were men who had seen what they had seen, and it would have been a miracle if they had not succumbed to the last temptation of virtuous spirits and fallen victims to some spiritual pride, assuming, moreover, the air of being the last Romans left alive. The Athenian citizen who voted for the banishment of Aristides said he did not know anything of that statesman, but it irritated him to hear him everywhere called " the just." And then there was Bright. Bright had been made member for Manchester in 1847, as a reward for his services to the cause of Free Trade. He had been a nuisance to three Liberal Prime Ministers, to Lord John Russell, to Lord Aberdeen, and Lord Palmerston. He had been violently opposed to the Crimean War. It must be admitted that Bright's conception of the part of a conscientious objector was extremely austere. His was not the politer spirit which declines any part in actual hostilities but puts in double time with work of national importance. He washed his hands of the whole business, and would have no more to do with the curing than the killing.

In this frame of mind he and Cobden approached, in 1857, their respective constituents of Manchester and the West Riding. In Manchester the Liberal party was split into two equal halves. The Palmerston Liberals tried to secure Robert Lowe, but eventually selected as their candidates Sir John Potter and Mr. Aspinwall Turner. Bright was seriously ill during the election in Italy, and Milner Gibson, his colleague in the representation of Manchester, bore the brunt of the fighting, with occasional help from Cobden who paid flying visits from Huddersfield. The *Guardian*, in strong and sometimes harsh terms, supported Potter and Turner, and was bitterly reproached by Cobden. As many Conservatives voted for the Palmerston candidates as were necessary to determine the result. The news

94

was sent to Bright in Venice. He was at the bottom of the poll, with Milner Gibson also defeated. Cobden, who had had the influence of the *Leeds Mercury* against him, as Bright had had that of the *Manchester Guardian*, went down in the West Riding. Fox was thrown out at Oldham, Sir Elkanah Armitage at Salford, and Miall, the leader of the forty Dissenters then in Parliament, was rejected at Rochdale. Most of them were quickly returned to Parliament. In a few weeks Birmingham had snapped up Bright, and in securing Bright secured also the Liberal lead for the next thirty years of politics.

The correspondence of Cobden was sore and sombre for many weeks on this subject of Manchester. He saw the beginnings of a new feudalism in Portland Street.

The honest and independent course taken by the people at Birmingham, their exemption from aristocratic snobbery, and their fair appreciation of a democratic son of the people confirm me in the opinion I have always had that the social and political state of that town is far more healthy than that of Manchester ; and it arises from the fact that the industry of the hardware district is carried on by small manufacturers, employing a few men and boys each, sometimes only an apprentice or two ; whilst the great capitalists of Manchester form an aristocracy, individual members of which wield an influence over sometimes two thousand persons. The former state of society is more natural and healthy in a moral and political sense. There is a freer intercourse between all classes than in the Lancashire town, where a great and impassable gulf separates the workman from his employer. The great capitalist class formed an excellent basis for the Anti-Corn Law movement, for they had inexhaustible purses which they opened freely in a contest where not only their pecuniary interests but their pride as " an order " was at stake. But I very much doubt whether such a state of society is favourable to a democratic political movement. . . . If Bright should recover his health and be able to head a party for Parliamentary reform, in my opinion Birmingham will be a better home for him than Manchester.

The election of 1857 is interesting for the first glimpse it gives us of the coming age of Manchester Liberalism. On Bright's platform at the Free Trade Hall appeared John Slagg, and the name of John Slagg carries us down to the fabulous eighties. We are plainly approaching the days of the gravelled drives of Victoria Park and Prestwich ; of the carriages with two horses which flashed their owners to great ovations at public meetings and carried them home through the torch-lighted night of victory and, not infrequently, defeat at the polls ; of the men who sat in the wide-back pews of Dissenting chapels and received the ministrations of Guinness Rogers, entertained Dr. Dale when he came to preach, were chosen by Mr. Gladstone to second the Address, and were, in short, the individuals produced by Individualism. We shall see the white hats of these Gladstonians and the side whiskers dimly distinguishable on the coasts of their powerful, sagacious faces. We have heard of John Slagg already, and at any moment we might come across Hugh Mason or Henry Lee. Or Leake and Agnew !

§ II

The *Guardian* fought the election of 1857 as a daily paper. This large development occurred in 1855 ; it was one of the many results of the high social constructivity of the Gladstonian Budgets. In 1853 Mr. Gladstone abolished the duty on soap and reduced 133 other taxes, giving a total remission of taxation of over five millions, and Milner Gibson carried against the Government a motion for the repeal of the advertisement duty, which now stood at eighteenpence. In 1855 the last penny of the newspaper duty was repealed. The duty on paper survived until 1861. It was the last of the " taxes on knowledge," and its abolition caused a constitutional crisis, the House of Lords making not certainly the last, but the last but one of its attempts to block the progress of a Money Bill. But the relief of 1855 was sufficient to ripen the *Guardian* to the full perfections of the daily status. The issue of June 16, 1855, contains the following announcement :

The bill for the abolition of the compulsory stamp duty on newspapers has now passed both Houses of Parliament and only waits the Royal Assent. We are therefore able to announce that the Daily Publication of the *Guardian* will commence on Monday the second of July next. The price, when unstamped, will be, as we have already stated, Twopence, instead of fivepence as at present ; in other words, we shall furnish our readers with six papers per week for a shilling instead of two for tenpence.

On July 2, 1855, the change was accordingly made, and two years later, in 1857, the price was reduced to one penny. The intelligence actively behind these critical operations was that of the second John Edward Taylor, who had now settled in Manchester and was taking his part in newspaper management in a period of great quickening. In 1861, on the retirement of Mr. Garnett (who died at Sale in 1870), he entered upon the undivided control of the paper. The full concert-pitch of London journalism became the object of his management. As early as 1856 the *Guardian* had made a great effort to secure a better report of Parliament. In this it failed, and for several years yet it had to be content with the report prepared for all the provincial papers by the Intelligence Department of the monopolistic telegraph companies. The report of Mr. Gladstone's Budget speech of 1860 sent out by this agency was a scandal of inefficiency, and all the provincial press agitated strongly for the nationalization of the telegraphs. In 1870, however, Mr. Taylor took the leading part in a newspaper development of great importance— the establishment of the Press Association. In 1868 the *Guardian* rented from the Post Office two private wires, opened a London office, and obtained entrance for its descriptive writer into the Gallery of the House of Commons. The

London Letter began, and numbered among its earliest contributors Tom Taylor, the dramatist and friend of Thackeray, who afterwards became editor of *Punch* ; M'Cullagh Torrens, the member for Finsbury ; and Tom Hughes, the author of *Tom Brown's School Days*.

The *Guardian* showed even greater enterprise in the following year, when the Franco-German War began. Mr. Taylor appointed and despatched his own staff of war correspondents. One of them was Mr. G. T. Robinson, an architect, the art-critic of the paper, and the father of the poetess, Mary F. Robinson, afterwards Madame Darmesteter and now Madame Duclaux. Another was General Cluseret. Robinson, who was shut up in Metz, and improvised a method of sending his messages out of the city by balloons, afterwards published a book on his experiences. The war service of the *Manchester Guardian* stood comparison with that of the London papers. The morning trains into Manchester were as early and as well informed as the morning trains into London, and at the close of the Franco-German War the *Guardian* had a national name.

Mr. John Edward Taylor, who in 1861 had married the youngest daughter of Mr. R. W. Warner, of Thetford, Norfolk, presided over these large operations partly from Manchester and partly from London, where he had gone to live. The editorship in Manchester went for a few years virtually into commission. Mr. R.

Dowman, a man of much curious learning, who is still remembered for the accomplishment of writing the whole of a long leader on a single slip of paper, took a large share of editorial duty. Another share was taken by Mr. John Couper, who lived until modern times, and whose beauty of character, coupled with great journalistic piety and the further circumstance that he acted as a sort of " father " to Mr. Scott in his early days of editorship, have canonized him in Cross Street. A third part was taken by Mr. H. M. Acton (the father of Mr. Justice Acton), a man of scholarship and wit, though somewhat cramped as a writer by his own severe classical standards, and yet another part by Mr. J. M. Maclean, who had already won distinction as editor of the *Bombay Gazette*, and was later still to exhibit to Parliament the spectacle of a Conservative member gravely embarrassed by persistent Liberal views. Mr. R. W. Spencer, who was at one time chief reporter and for many years the chief sub-editor of the paper, joined it about this time. He was a man of much ability and judgment, and his long tenure of an important position in its service counted for a great deal in the progress of the *Guardian*. Mr. Peter Allen, brother-in-law of the second John Edward Taylor and the father of Mr. Russell Allen, the present proprietor of the *Manchester Evening News*, was the shrewd and genial business manager. Mr. G. V. Marsh had succeeded John Harland in the office of chief reporter. The *Guardian* was a daily paper, but there still clung to it some of the atmosphere of its bi-weekly days. It was the product of long, leisurely afternoons. Its leader-writers withheld their hands from the news of the current night, and went home, like barristers, on reasonable evening trains.

VI : *THE HAPPY LIBERALS*

CHAPTER VI

The Happy Liberals

§ I

IT was among the men, and into the conditions described in the last chapter, that there arrived in 1871 a new editorial recruit in the person of Charles Prestwich Scott.

The present proprietor and editor of the *Manchester Guardian* was born at Bath in 1846. His father and his grandfather were both named Russell Scott. His grandfather was the Rev. Russell Scott, a well-known Unitarian minister, who was for forty-five years in charge of the High Street Chapel at Portsmouth, and was a sort of bishop of his denomination. To the Rev. Russell Scott three children were born. The eldest died in infancy. The second one, Sophia Russell Scott, has already entered into our narrative as the first wife of John Edward Taylor, the founder of the *Manchester Guardian*. Charles Prestwich Scott is therefore the nephew by marriage of John Edward Taylor, and has a more distant blood relationship with him arising from the circumstance that John Edward Taylor and his wife were first cousins.

The third child of the Rev. Russell Scott was a son, Russell Scott. He became a merchant in London, and married Isabella Prestwich, a woman of much beauty and talent, who lived at her father's house in South Lambeth, though she was descended from an old Manchester family settled at one time at Hulme Hall. Her brother, Sir Joseph Prestwich, became Professor of Geology at Oxford, and she herself, ending her days at Denton, near to Manchester, is well remembered there for her devoted spirit and by the social and educational institutions which she gave to the place. Russell Scott succeeded in business. He retired in early middle life, and devoted himself to the education of a large family and to philanthropy. It was largely by his assistance that Miss Mary Carpenter established, in 1852, the Kingswood Reformatory School near Bristol, one of the first institutions of its kind in the country, and the management of this school occupied much of his time during the years in which he lived with his family at Bath. Charles Prestwich Scott is the eighth of his nine children, of whom the ninth died in infancy. His eldest brother, Russell Scott, who died in 1908, was a merchant in London, and a steady and generous friend of the Liberal party and of many good causes. Another brother, the Rev. Lawrence Scott, has for many years been the Unitarian minister at Denton.

Charles Prestwich Scott was educated at private schools and by a private tutor in the Isle of Wight. One of his masters was the Rev. Joseph Hutton, brother of R. H. Hutton, of the *Spectator*, and another, the Rev. Charles Pritchard, afterwards professor of astronomy at Cambridge.

His Nonconformist descent and his own Non-conformist attitude—for he refused to be bound to attend college chapel, though in point of fact he always went—were a difficulty in the way of his entrance to one of the old univer-sities, but in 1865 he obtained admission to Corpus Christi, Oxford, on the result of the scholarship examination, no difficulty being raised against him at that very liberal college. His recreation at the University was rowing, and in his last year he was captain of his college boat. He left Oxford in 1869 with a first in " Greats " and an invitation from his cousin, the second John Edward Taylor, to join the staff of the *Manchester Guardian.* As a further and more definite preparation for his work in Manchester he went to Edinburgh and served for a year in the office of the *Scotsman,* under the illustrious Alexander Russel. In the spring of 1871 he came to Manchester just in time to be present at the festivities which celebrated the jubilee of the *Manchester Guardian.* In 1872, at the age of twenty-five, Mr. Scott entered upon the editorship which has enriched and ornamented all Liberal causes the world over, and which, continuing to this day, not only without failure or abatement, but with a still continued ripening and expansion of powers, promises to endow humanity with another example of the courage and capacity of advanced years, and to add one more name to the world's list of grand old men.

Mr. Scott was married in 1874 to Miss Rachel

Susan Cook, the daughter of Dr. John Cook, professor of ecclesiastical history in the University of St. Andrews and one time Moderator of the Established Church of Scotland. Mrs. Scott was one of the seven original students of the College for Women at Hitchin, which afterwards developed into Girton College, Cambridge. She took the Cambridge Classical Tripos with a distinction which was not equalled for some time by any other woman student. On her marriage with Mr. Scott she came to live in Manchester, and gave all the powers she could to the service of the city. She was one of the founders of the College in Brunswick Street for the Higher Education of Women, which is now merged in the Manchester University. She succeeded Miss Becker on the Manchester School Board. Mrs. Scott was in intimate touch with her husband's editorial work, was with him in all the decisions, and particularly the decisions on the Irish question in 1886 and the South African question in 1899, which liberalized the *Guardian*, and she had much to do with developing and improving the department of book-reviewing, which began to grow famous in her time.

Mrs. Scott died in 1905, but her influence has lived on in the subsequent history of the paper, and her spirit, critical yet enthusiastic, is ingrained in its spirit. There is a memory of her which is still probably treasured among the moral possessions of some who were present at the historic meeting in the St. James's Hall,

Manchester, in the autumn of 1899, called to protest against the South African War. She was then deeply worn by the heavy physical sufferings of her last years, but she was present at that meeting, and in the company of the son of Bright and the daughter of Gladstone she took with Morley, Courtney and her husband all her share of its martyrdoms. She went through the ordeal of the night seeming hardly a corporeal presence at all ; rather a flame of pure spirit—purified.

Mr. and Mrs. Scott's daughter married Mr. C. E. Montague, who joined the editorial staff of the paper from Balliol in 1890, and is accounted one of the highest ornaments of English journalism. Their eldest son, Lawrence Prestwich Scott, died in 1908. He had been on the editorial staff of the paper for seven years, and was promising to contribute high moral and intellectual qualities to the enrichment of its future history. Two other sons, John Russell Scott and Edward Taylor Scott, are in the service of the paper, the former as its business manager, the latter as a leader-writer giving special attention to economic questions.

§ II

The opening of the London office and the private wire, the appointment of a Parliamentary writer, the despatch of war correspondents armed with blank cheques to the Franco-German War, and the appointment of Mr. C. P. Scott are a group of events standing in a close circle around the year 1868, and it was in this year also that the Liberal party arose, new and splendid, out of the shattered fragments of the Whigs, the Peelites, the Palmerstonians, and the Manchester School. For the next eighteen years a party composed of all these elements, and socially so catholic that it included dukes and included dustmen, was to find its full satisfaction and felicity, its bond of union and well of inspiration, in the matchless public and private character of Mr. Gladstone. The political Nonconformists, the Congregationalists, the Baptists, and Unitarians, and all their prophets and pastors, their Dales, Parkers, Spurgeons, McLarens, and Martineaus, were of this party to a man, Mr. Forster's Education Act vexing them but not permanently driving them away. There was a liberal sprinkling of eminent Churchmen. Jowett, of Balliol, belonged to it, and when the first working miner appeared in Parliament in the person of Thomas Burt, he also was of it.

Its principal opponents were Beer and Bible, the alliance of which was much commented upon during and after the election of 1874. At the hands of Beer and Bible the Liberal party of those days sustained heavy and bitter defeats, but these experiences were only the beating of the weather outside the house. There was warmth and company inside. There was no little self-righteousness. Dr. Dale, who bitterly lamented the break-up of the Liberal party in 1886, has said somewhere that it had ceased to be a party and had become a church. It was richer than almost any party has been before or since in leadership. Its members of the rank and file sat them down beneath a canopy of character and genius which could muster the organ tones of morals and politics or admit beams of celestial light. When Mr. Gladstone threatened to retire from the leadership in 1876, Bright, Forster, Lowe, and Hartington were his companions on the front Opposition bench, and each one was a possible leader. Harcourt and Henry James were not thought weighty enough. Chamberlain and Dilke were a little too young. Mr. Gladstone's retirement did not last long. In two or three years the Eastern Question arose, and a perfectly new phenomenon known as a " Midlothian campaign," heated up by railway station oratory at every stopping-place between Queensferry and Edinburgh, arose in English politics, not a little to the perturbation of Queen Victoria, who took grave exception to this apotheosis of a subject. Liberal associations assembled on railway platforms towards noon, enjoyed two minutes of concentrated lion-gazing, and dispersed when the train moved on, totally unfitted for the business of the rest of the day. The *Manchester Guardian*, besides reporting Mr. Gladstone, took to describing him. In 1880 local members of Parliament were telling their audiences that Mr. Gladstone had reached his seventieth year. After that he became legendary. Elderly men were presented by their families at Christmas with the acceptable gift of a piece of wood guaranteed by the dealer to be a chip from his axe. In the last years of his life he did little to alter or modify the system of England, but the example of these years kept her soul alive.

In circumstances like these the problems of Liberal editorship with which Mr. Scott had to deal in his first ten years of office were not difficult. But the second Gladstonian Government, of 1880, had not been in power very long when it became apparent that a fissure was developing in the Liberal party. On the one side were Hartington, Goschen, and the Whigs ; on the other, Chamberlain and the Midland Radicals and the impatient youth of the party. These two sections began to manœuvre against one another for the control of the next few years of politics. Chamberlain became the hero of provincial Liberalism, though there are many elderly Liberals living to-day who can boast that they never liked him, and can quote the very words they used to this effect in the street outside his most spell-bound meetings. He concocted an " unauthorized programme " which promised the Liberal party not only years of office but, what is even more important to a party, work to do while it was in office. It was totally to re-shape the rural life of England, a work in which all Radical manufacturers, all people who lived themselves in cities and towns, and indeed everybody except landlords, squires, and clergymen, could join with the utmost satisfaction to his party interests and no personal risk to his private status and fortune, however far the process went. The new rural constituencies responded by returning many Liberal members at the election of 1885. Mr. Gladstone chose this moment of moments in party history to be converted to Home Rule. He put the Nonconformist masses of the Liberal party to a severe trial of faith and temper. Instead of uprooting the land laws and disestablishing the Church, they were to face the prospect of twenty years of opposition for the sake of a people whom they knew to be Papists and suspected to be reactionaries.

Large mental readjustments had to be made. It was not only that Chamberlain turned against his maker and that Bright forsook his great brother. In a year or two it became known that the Duke of Westminster had sold the Millais portrait of Mr. Gladstone for money. The Liberal party in those six months of crisis sustained many losses and made few gains. One of its gains was the *Manchester Guardian*. In the years between 1880 and 1885 the *Guardian* had been totally unattracted by the metallic Radicalism of Birmingham. It was still governed by its old Whig bias, and leaned definitely towards Hartington and Goschen. If the sons of the most strait-laced Liberalism will throw back their minds to this period they will find the *Manchester Examiner and Times*, and not the

Manchester Guardian, in the furniture of old associations, and heralding at home the new-born day. The *Guardian* might have been expected with certainty to follow Hartington into a Whig secession. Its long habit of extreme caution in politics seemed to prepare it for this course ; the weather at the moment recommended it. All through the winter of 1885, and the spring of 1886, it can be heard thinking aloud on this Irish question in its leading columns. It disagreed with Mr. Gladstone's first thoughts on the exclusion of the Irish members, but its conversion to the principle of Home Rule went forward day by day. " Against the transfer to an Irish assembly of full practical control of Irish affairs we have not a word to say. That is the essence of Home Rule as we understand it, and Home Rule even in this large sense we are prepared to accept. The fundamental objection to the Bill lies in the exclusion of the Irish members," etc. (April 9, 1886.) " There can be no question now of denying a measure of Home Rule." (April 10.) " At whatever disadvantage, with whatever loss, the Liberal party must go forward with a work perhaps the most imperative and salutary which ever divolved upon it in its history." (June 9, after the defeat of the Bill.) While editorial opinion was setting into this mould, Professor Freeman, in another part of the paper, was explaining the historical and political *rational* of Mr. Gladstone's policy in a series of signed articles.

At the same moment of time the *Manchester Examiner* hesitated, and, in the event, was lost. Mr. Gladstone's conversion to Home Rule was often described by Mr. Gladstone's critics as the sharp curve of politics. The *Manchester Examiner* was one of the accidents. For rather more than thirty years it had been edited by Henry Dunckley, and during the whole of this period it had been the authentic voice of the Manchester school of politics. Henry Dunckley, who had been a Nonconformist minister in Salford, was chosen to edit the *Examiner* because he won a prize offered by the Anti-Corn Law League, in 1854, for an essay on the history and results of its agitation. The essay was a masterpiece, and Dunckley's editorship of the *Examiner* was an affair of much political and literary distinction. He wrote a style of great strength and of such simplicity that his readers vowed they had never needed to read a sentence twice however subtle the thought, and he was not a man to whom subtlety never happened. It is just possible that as an editor he was a little too sedentary even for the quiet days in which his lot was cast. People who remember him in his office speak of his velvet jacket and cigar, and the sanctity of his meditations. They say that in the *Examiner* office a housekeeper in a black alpaca used to go about at ten at night administering tea to the stylists and the thinkers. They also say that the *Examiner* missed the Tay Bridge accident, the sub-editors having all joined at a cab home shortly after the first tidings of the disaster arrived, and that the editor thought the excuse not an unreasonable one, seeing that it had certainly been snowing hard. Only once was he known to indulge an editor's right to tear his hair and rend his garments. As one of the most important Liberals in the country, it fell to him during a crisis to attend a momentous conference of the party in London. Suspecting himself to be the only journalist present, he spent the evening composing and wiring to the office in Manchester a discreet but nevertheless highly inspired and intimate account of what had happened, and followed it up with a private telegram to the sub-editor informing him that the message was what would now be called " exclusive." It did not appear, and when Dunckley, on his return to Manchester, asked why it had not appeared, he received the following reasoned reply : " Well, sir, it was this way. I was much pressed for space and, as you had yourself said that the other papers would not have anything about the conference, I thought I might safely leave it all out." Dunckley appears to have thought that a journalistic mind of this sort had better exercise itself for the rest of its career in an office which was not his office. And it did.

It is certain that for one reason and another the *Examiner* ran to tops rather than roots. But Dunckley's hold on Liberal England was extremely strong. He acquired it with a series

of articles in the *Weekly Times*, an offshoot of
the *Examiner*, on the exact status of the Crown
in the English Constitution, a subject on which
Radical opinion had been much poked up by
certain objectionable passages in Sir Theodore
Martin's *Life of the Prince Consort*. The
Quarterly Review handled Dunckley severely
for these articles, and his reply made the controversy illustrious. By the time it was con-
cluded it had become obvious that the " Letters
of Verax " must be continued, and in their con-
tinuation they roamed over all the field of politics
and touched frequently on those questions of
political theology which were always burning
while England was still ruled by its Nonconformist chapels. It was said that they were
even more read in the West Riding of Yorkshire
than in Lancashire, instructing great masses
of the electorate and sometimes turning by-
elections.

Many people habitually swore by Dunckley.
If you saw it in a " Letter of Verax," it was
so. There have been few writers who have
been more read by people who read nothing
else but the Book of the Prophet Isaiah, and
indeed the wonderful thing about Henry Dunckley was not so much Henry Dunckley himself
—historian and scholar, stylist and ironist though
he was—as his public, and not so much the
plant as the highly indoctrinated soil in which
it grew. His fame was his own, but it was
also one of the achievements of the North of

England. After all, they also write who only put on their spectacles and trim the lamp to read and consider.

Largely under the influence of John Bright, who had been one of its founders, the *Examiner* missed the tide of Liberal sentiment in 1886. It got away with the next tide. In a few weeks it had " found salvation," but the delay damaged it, and it never quite recovered. Three years later it was sold to the Liberal Unionist party, and the *Guardian* acquired nearly all its public goodwill in acquiring the services of Dunckley, who began in March, 1889, to contribute a weekly article under his familiar name of " Verax." These articles were continued until his death in 1896, and assisted greatly in bringing the old *Examiner* readers over to the *Guardian* and making them at home in its columns. Dunckley also wrote a good deal for the *Guardian* which was not signed. The obituary notice of Mr. Gladstone in 1898 had been largely written by him before his own death.

§ III

William Thomas Arnold had become a strong influence in the *Guardian* office when the decision on Home Rule was taken in 1886, and indeed Arnold's best years as a journalist were spent on the Irish question. He was the grandson of Arnold of Rugby and the brother of Mrs. Humphry Ward. Mr. Scott visited Oxford in 1879 in search of an editorial recruit, dis-

WILLIAM THOMAS ARNOLD.

covered Arnold, and brought him back to Manchester. From that year until 1896, when he was attacked by the illness which finally terminated his brilliant and beautiful life, Arnold was an active and powerful member of the editorial staff, and for the second part of the period the chief leader-writer. He has a very high place in the *Guardian* calendar, and might be named with Scott and Montague as one of the chief modern makers of the paper. Arnold was an historian. He was, in point of fact, a specialist in Roman provincial administration, and it was because he gave so much of his life to journalism that his historical writing forms only a fragment, valuable as that fragment is. The journalist, in fact, spoiled the historian, but the historian perfected the journalist. It was Arnold's own theory that his journalism in the *Guardian* office was all the better for his historical studies at his house in Nelson Street, and that the morning and evening thus spent made the day. It is certain that this absorption in a very lonely field of historical research did nothing to stale his interest in modern politics and in the local affairs of Manchester. It merely added the critical habit of mind and a slight touch of occasional " donnishness." To some extent he shared Macaulay's amiable delusion about the current " schoolboy," and he was prone to suppose not only that everybody had read Mommsen, but that everybody kept his own copy of Mommsen on a convenient shelf.

But as a practical, serviceable journalist of the small hours Arnold has rarely been equalled. Knowing everything about something (Roman inscriptions), he had the further ambition of knowing something about everything. He was the architect of a system of " pigeon-holes " which were contrived to serve the cause, not indeed of omniscience, but of a kind of omnia-consciousness. His own room at the *Guardian* office was elaborately equipped with " pigeon-holes," and was the scene of an incessant alighting of doves from the most remote climates of the foreign reviews, from the cycling papers, from the medical, the ironmongery, and grocery papers, and indeed from everywhere and anywhere where " the facts " about any subject under the sun could be collected—virginal and unimpassioned. Mr. Montague has minutely described this method in a chapter of great journalistic edification in the Arnold memoir.

At his house in Nelson Street, the site and garden of which were absorbed into the new Royal Infirmary, Arnold became a local patriot. He made the great spiritual discovery that there was no need to go to London, and that a region bounded by the Pennine Range on the east and by Blackpool promenade on the west could neither be outwritten nor outgrown. He may be taken as the true founder of the *genre* school of *Guardian* writers, a body as defined and distinguishable in its way as the Glasgow school of art. The drama of the town, and even in course of time its music-halls of Empire and Hippo-drome, its picture galleries and loan exhibitions, its concerts, its Whit-week, its Zoological Gardens at Belle Vue, and all its encircling scenery of Cheshire and Derbyshire became, under the stimulus of his first example, the subject matter of a critical attitude, a descriptiveness and a habit of hard writing resolving themselves into a family style highly literary but never bookish, and the spiritual secret of which is a slight dis-dain of London, an austere contentment with the object before the eye, and a grim determina-tion to write before the end of life more or less like Montague. One of the earliest-gathered fruits of the school was a little volume on the Manchester stage. It consisted of dramatic criticisms in the columns of the *Guardian* by Mr. Arnold, Mr. Montague, Mr. Oliver Elton, and Mr. Allan Monkhouse, and its modest and unassuming appearance in the world was yet an event in the literary treatment of the theatre. Mr. Arthur Johnstone, a musical critic and im-pressionist of great brilliance, carried the move-ment on from this starting-point. Mr. J. B. Atkins, now of the *Spectator*, but formerly the war correspondent of the *Guardian* in several campaigns, developed the *Guardian* style con-siderably on the side of social and descriptive writing first in Manchester and afterwards in London. It was the achievement of Mr. Atkins to carry the Puritan reader not unenjoyably to the race meeting at Doncaster or Epsom.

These earlier efforts were made behind the curtain of anonymity, but the school of writers which grew up around Arnold, and found in Montague at once its example and despair, became rather too big for anonymity. It broke through. Initials were admitted. They became recognizable and known, and several journalists in Manchester acquired the boulevardish fame of their brothers in Paris. It became the regular thing that a dramatic audience in Manchester should enjoy two performances for every play— the one in the theatre itself, the other the next morning in the *Guardian*, when the critic recited the adventure of his own soul in the presence of the masterpiece, or the hollow thing of brass and tinsel, as the case might be.

Long before the growth of this local school of criticism the *Guardian* had been collecting specialists more particularly for the reviewing of books. We have already named Professor Freeman as a contributor, but the paper has always helped itself liberally from historical scholarship. Mandell Creighton was writing reviews and leading articles for the *Guardian* steadily before he became the Bishop of Peterborough. Goldwin Smith was a frequent contributor. York Powell is one of the treasures which the *Guardian* has stolen from time to time from what is still called the higher literature. The men who asked one another in the common rooms and at the hall tables of Oxford why York Powell did not put forth more books could have found the answer in the innumerable anonymous articles which he was writing for the *Manchester Guardian*. He was a constant contributor of historical essays written around and about any book sent to him for review, and a large part of the small but valuable completed output of that remarkable writer is to be found in the columns of the *Guardian* of his day. Among other regular writers were Andrew Lang and Richard Jefferies (the natural historian). Mr. George Saintsbury, the critic, was on the resident editorial staff in the seventies, and was a contemporary in the office with Mr. Richard Whiteing, the novelist. Mr. Spenser Wilkinson joined the editorial staff in 1882, and continued to be a member of it for ten years. Mr. John Masefield (for a brief period) and Mr. Filson Young are old members of the staff, and Stanley Houghton, the author of *Hindle Wakes*, contributed the signed articles which now form part of his collected works, and was a constant writer of theatrical criticism. Professor L. T. Hobhouse joined the editorial staff in 1898, and brought with him from Mr. Scott's old college at the University, of which he was a Fellow, a splendid combination of a wide philosophical outlook, of which his books on political and sociological subjects give ample evidence, together with an ardent and reasoned Liberalism and the mastery of an accomplished style. Mr. T. M. Young, now the Deputy Public Trustee, was for some time the city editor. Mr. William Archer was for several years in charge of the London dramatic criticism. Mr. R. A. M. Stevenson, Mr. Comyns Carr, Sir Claude Phillips, Mr. D. S. MacColl, Sir Walter Armstrong, Mr. Laurence Housman, and Mr. Sturge Moore have been included in its very strong succession of art critics in London. Sir Arthur Evans, the well-known traveller and archæologist, did some brilliant work for it in connection with his archæological surveys in the old Venetian lands on the Eastern Adriatic, and was for a time imprisoned by the Austrians because of his advocacy of the liberties of the local population. Later, Mr. Amery, now Under Secretary for the Colonies, acting as correspondent of the *Guardian* in the same disturbed region, ran great risk of being run through the body by a Turkish zaptieh whom he up and smote with his umbrella in the assertion of his rights as a British subject to go and do what he pleased. Long ago the paper gave to the public much of the original writings of Ben Brierley and Edwin Waugh, of the Lancashire school of writers.

The *Guardian* has found many regular contributors in the professorate of the Manchester University. Sir Adolphus Ward, the former Principal of the University, and now the Master of Peterhouse, Cambridge, was the earliest of its distinguished dramatic critics, and has been a frequent reviewer down even to the present day. Sir Henry Roscoe, Professor Munroe, Mr. Balfour's persevering opponent in East Manchester and a great adornment in his time of local Liberalism, Professor Wilkins, and, in the present day, Professor Herford are among the names of its contributors. Among the ecclesiastics who have written regularly on Church questions have been Professor Hope Moulton and Canon Hicks, afterwards Bishop of Lincoln, whose place as the writer of a weekly article on affairs from a Churchman's point of view was taken, and is still held, by Canon Peter Green. Mr. H. W. Massingham and Mr. Harold Spender have represented the *Guardian* in Parliament, and Mr. H. W. Nevinson has acted for it as a war correspondent and has been a steady contributor. Mr. R. H. Gretton, the historian of modern England, was formerly in charge of the London office. Mr. G. W. E. Russell began in 1897, and continued for many years, in the *Guardian* his recollections of the Whig society of the Victorian age. The late Mr. Dixon Scott, Mr. G. H. Mair (who was probably the first journalist in England to make an aeroplane flight), Mr. Ernest Newman, Mr. John Drinkwater, Mr. Harold Brighouse, Mr. Clutton Brock, Mr. J. A. Hobson, Mr. H. N. Brailsford, Mr. Lowes Dickinson, Mr. J. E. Agate, Mr. J. L. Hammond, and (in the most recent times) Mr. Maurice Hewlett, Mr. R. H. Tawney, and Mr. J. M. Keynes are among the many authors and critics who have found their journalistic outlet in the columns of the *Manchester Guardian*. The present staff, which maintains all the old accustomed strength, includes Mr. W. P. Crozier, who has had much to do with the modernization of the paper, and Mr. James Bone, who combines the charge of the London office with the function of art critic. Mr. J. J. O'Neill, the late Liberal candidate for Preston, is the valued head of the advertisement branch of the paper. The " Miscellany " column, to which crowds of professional and amateur journalists have brought their offerings, began to appear in the autumn of 1903. Later on, the back-page article was established, and has become one of the standing targets of literary marksmanship.

VII : *THE SOUL OF A NEWSPAPER*

CHAPTER VII

The Soul of a Newspaper

§ I

THE Irish question was to the *Manchester Guardian* literally, and in no figure of speech, a Liberal education. Gladstonianism began with the Irish question, but it transcended it. It developed into a political attitude and mentality which we describe when we say that it is of all things in the world the precise and exact opposite of Prussianism. It called upon the ruler to put himself imaginatively into the place of the ruled. It became a feeling for the nationality of other people. Still more to the point at which we have now arrived, it inured those who followed it to the unpleasant process of thinking and acting against the grain of a facile patriotism, and living in allegiance to that other country which is also theirs and is bounded on the north, the south, the east and the west, not by political frontiers, but by the moral idea. From Ireland to South Africa was a change of scene, but hardly a change of mind, and the statesman who had most to do with the defeat of the two Home Rule Bills was also the statesman who brought a restless and aggressive Imperialism on to the scene of affairs. The *Manchester Guardian* itself was about to enter upon a chapter in which it was set inflexibly against the national will. A new and highly inconvenient patriotic exercise known as " giving up the *Guardian* " was soon to be seen practised for the first time in first-class carriages running into Manchester. It was often performed with great pomp and circumstance ; newsagents, who were not responsible for the opinions of the paper, being addressed on the subject across their counters as though they were public meetings. There are some who cherish to this day the simple child-like faith that the *Guardian* takes foreign money, and would be left almost helpless in controversy with it if told that it is even not so. The paper needed all its roots in the family life of Manchester, in its commerce, its markets, its churches, its music and art and sport to survive the weather which beat upon it during the South African War. But these roots held well enough, and it is a curious but reassuring fact that many people, after " giving up the *Guardian* " for one offence, were found to be in a position to " give it up " again somewhat later, the circumstance affording some evidence of a secret reconciliation in the meantime.

It is not often that we find such sharp departures in history, but if England had only known it, she was hearing, when she heard the news of the Jameson Raid, of the end of her peace. Since that event the world has known no rest. It was the first sudden symptom of a deep disorder. If English politics before 1896 be compared with English politics since 1896, it will be seen that a change in the character of public questions took place about that year. Before 1896 politics were concerned very largely with man as an Anglican or Baptist, with man as a teetotaller or not a teetotaller, with man as a single or peradventure a plural voter. Theology entered very largely into politics. Large masses of people voted one way or the other according as they were or were not of a Puritan strain. Someone before 1896 had compiled a *Handbook to the Political Questions of the Day*, and, if this book be examined, it will be found that the arguments, *pro* and *con*, are marshalled on a number of questions, most of them having this common characteristic : that no one would be one penny the better or worse whatever the decision. Should the Church in Wales be disestablished and disendowed ; should the Church in England ; should the inhabitants of a given area have the power to determine whether there should be any, and, if so, how many, licences for the sale of intoxicating drink ; should the Bible be taught in schools to whose support Jews and agnostics were compelled to contribute—was it possible to teach the Bible without doctrinal comment ? The argument of these questions by recognized gladiators was the characteristic feature of English life. It was as typical of England as the bull-fight is of Spain. It is a curious fact that while hardly one of these questions was settled by the disputants, they have nearly all by now settled themselves. The education question, for example, which was not an education question at all, but a theological one, has totally evaporated in a new climate of affairs. It has been settled not by consent, but by default. When it was last before the court no one appeared on either side, and the case was struck out of the list.

The two armies of Liberal and Conservative, the Montagues and the Capulets of Church and Dissent, had very little idea what a large mass of the population it was that took little or no interest in their contentions and very much preferred the racecourse. The Jameson Raid was the signal for these people to join in. The game of African Imperialism had begun, and it was a game which everybody could understand. It was felt that this was going to be as good as hunting. The Jameson raiders were brought to London for their trial, and were severely scolded by Lord Russell of Killowen, but their sunburnt faces and extremely smart neckties made a deep impression on the new attentive England. The Jameson raiders having been duly punished and petted, Mr. Chamberlain raised the claim to the suzerainty of the Transvaal, and began with great dexterity to manœuvre President Kruger and the Boer farmers, through the mazes of the five years franchise and the seven years franchise, to the verge of the precipice over which they eventually slipped. "More and more," wrote Mr. C. P. Scott, from the *Guardian* office to Leonard Courtney, about this time in a letter published in Courtney's life—" more and more one feels that foreign policy is the touchstone of all policy."

Political Imperialism was succeeded by economic Imperialism. When Mr. Chamberlain began his fiscal campaign he was mainly an Imperialist, and only incidentally a Protectionist, but the Imperialism was quickly brushed on one side, large and powerful interests having seen in the other aspect of the question what they would in their own language call a " business proposition " of the highest interest and importance. These were indeed practical politics ! The country gave the movement a severe check at the election of 1906, but a period of great secret activity followed in foreign politics. The striking fall in the tone of public life which had now taken place was indicated when the Irish question was raised after an interval of fifteen years, and the responsible leaders of the Unionist party identified themselves cordially with flat rebellion, and set an example which was followed right and left— by militant suffragists, and by Labour men who turned with disdain from the House of Commons and had no use even for the discipline of the old trade union. Then came the ripening of all these things in the European War. The new times which we have thus sketched had been served throughout their course by a new kind of press which was impatient of speeches and called voraciously morning after morning for events.

The notable part which the *Manchester Guardian* has played against the whole gamut of this movement was first definitely assumed in the days before the South African War, when the minority in England was watching with anguish the diplomatic performances of Mr. Chamberlain. The *Guardian* not only fought the battle in its leading articles, but it nourished into being the " Manchester Transvaal Committee," which called the historic meeting of protest at the St. James's Hall on September 15, 1899. It was a member of the staff of the *Manchester Guardian* who visited Lord Morley, then living at Hawarden, where he was writing the *Life of Gladstone*, and prevailed upon him to come. Mr. Scott himself summoned Courtney from Beachy Head. A son of Bright took the chair, and a daughter of Gladstone was on the platform. Lord Morley's own diaries describe the meeting, telling how he was met by apprehensive faces at the Exchange Station ; how the war party had publicly advertised and encouraged attempts to smash the meeting ; how young men had been earnestly exhorted in patriotic prints, at least for one night to sacrifice their billiards and tobacco for the honour of their native land ; how the huge St. James's Hall was packed as it had never been packed before, and how the chairman was ruthlessly shouted down.

But Lord Morley's account of the affair does

something less than justice to the courage of his own contention with the crowd, to the victory of mind over matter, inch by inch, sentence by sentence, here a little and there a little, but at last so complete that the closing words of his speech were heard in a silence the very unwillingness of which added, if anything could add, to their sombre beauty. They form one of the best examples modern speaking affords of the use of the great organ stop in politics.

I ask myself very often in my doctrinaire study whether the man with the sword blundering in and slashing at knots which patient statesmen might have untied is not responsible for half the worst catastrophes in the political history of Europe. Yes, you may carry fire and sword into the midst of peace and industry. Such a war of one of the strongest Governments of the world against this weak little Republic will bring you no glory. It will bring you no profit, but mischief. It will be wrong. It will make thousands of women widows and children fatherless. It will be wrong. You may add a new province to your Empire. It will still be wrong. You may give greater buoyancy to the South African stock markets. You may create South African booms. You may send the price of Mr. Rhodes's Chartereds to a point beyond the dreams of avarice. Yet even then it will still be wrong.

In less than a month of the uttering of these words war was declared. The *Guardian* placed on record its remonstrance.

No sane man among us can look back on all that has happened since the Jameson Raid and honestly deny that step by step the Boers have been driven to the dizzy edge of the precipice as systematically and mercilessly as ever a weak and weakly governed nation was driven by an adroit diplomatist wielding the resources of a great Power. We are now on the eve of the period when the discussion of the causes of the war is more or less silenced by the din of war itself. But it is something to have made it clear to the world, as the peace movement of the last few weeks has done, that this is a war into which the better part of England will enter with a heavy heart, with an upright man's regret and resentment at the conduct of agents who have placed him in an ignoble position, and with the most earnest hope that the struggle may be short, and that the early easy success of our forces may be followed by a peace in which some of the credit lost to us may be restored by a magnanimous use of our power.

This hope was eventually made good, though it was not to be foreseen when the words were written how and by whom. Dark days followed, and the lot of the peace party went from bad to worse as the war turned out to be, not the full-dress parade which had been expected, but a troublesome affair of money and time and lives. The *Guardian* office was often threatened with physical violence, and was sometimes under police protection, as, somewhat to his discontent, was Mr. Scott's own house. It is a chapter in the history of the *Manchester Guardian* which should be turned over with pleasure even by those who think the paper was wrong on the merits of the South African War. That the decision to oppose the war was taken without the smallest regard to the commercial interests of the paper is personal to the *Manchester Guardian* itself, but that the risk should have been run with perfect success reflects hopefully on the conditions of public life in England, and lights a lamp on the roadway of faith. A newspaper lives, and must live, by its advertisements and circulation, or by a combination of the two. There have been newspapers 'which have complained of this hard fact, and have held it responsible for the extinction of some truth which they would have liked to preach, but the world would not let them. It is, however, only an application of the truth that the soul needs first of all a body. The Word must become a sound and serviceable incarnation, and just as the highest spiritual life must be based on the humdrum virtues, and a man cannot be a saint of the Church if he snaps at his family at home or neglects to answer his letters, so a perfectly fearless and independent journalism must be based on great journalistic quality and temper.

It must, in fact, be well timbered. It must be able to get itself read, dullness being the one deadly sin against truth since it stops the ears of receptivity. It must learn, over a course of many years, to be depended on implicitly for the facts. It must know that there is a time to write and a time to refrain from writing, and that it is often the highest controversial wisdom to change the subject and to fall to talking with love and knowledge about a new bowler for the Lancashire team, the annual pantomime, or the Old Infirmary Site, or any other topic which arose before and will outlast the state of policy and parties. It must weave away at the plain homespun of reputation. Great affairs in their place, but not all over the place ! If a newspaper has these reserves of character and authority and versatility it will probably be able to give the world as much truth as it is able to bear. To give it more is to give it none. Such, at any rate, has been the experience of the *Manchester Guardian*. It was not for nothing that the first John Edward Taylor, whose politics disappointed so many of his friends, had yet the habit of looking twice at every paragraph before it appeared in the *Manchester Guardian*, and that the second John Edward Taylor added enterprise to truth. These things made possible its modern " liberty of prophesying " under Mr. C. P. Scott.

At the time of the South African War decisions of policy were, and for many years had been, in the keeping of Mr. Scott, but the ultimate ownership of the paper was still with Mr. John Edward Taylor. For many years Mr. Taylor had lived in London, and his visits to Manchester after 1870 were only occasional, though he figured prominently in Lancashire politics for a brief hour in 1874, when he stood unsuccessfully with Mr. Peter Rylands as Liberal candidate for the undivided constituency of South-east Lancashire, the association of the two men deriving some interest from the asso-

JOHN EDWARD TAYLOR,

Editor of the *Manchester Guardian* from 1861 till 1871 and proprietor until 1905.

ciation of their fathers, the one as the prisoner
at the bar and the other as foreman of the jury,
at the trial at Lancaster in 1819. As the proprietor of a newspaper, the second John Edward
Taylor had the high virtue of choosing an editor
wisely and then abiding by his choice. He was,
however, in the fullest sympathy with Mr.
Scott's decision on the South African War and
the even more momentous decision on the Irish
question. His own attitude towards the questions on which the *Guardian* made its mark
has been described by an intimate hand, the
words standing for him who wrote them almost
as well as for him about whom they were written :

. . . Mr. Taylor took a deep and abiding interest
in another great question affecting the lives of the
poor—that of temperance,—and his strong feeling
on this subject helped to stimulate and deepen his
convictions in the whole range of domestic politics.
Indeed, there took place with him a process the con-
verse of that commonly attributed to advancing years.
Age brought to him no weakening of popular sympathies, no narrowing of the outlook upon life ; above
all, no tolerance of high-handed wrong, whether committed by others or by ourselves. To the modern
materialism, to the new assertion of the ancient doctrine that might is right, to the plea for national
selfishness as the true guide of the policy of States,
he remained irreconcilably opposed, and, in the
strength of this antagonism, he was fired in his age
with something of the ardour of youth.

One other thing remains to be told of Mr.
Taylor. One day in 1873 he gave the order

that from that day and thenceforward racing
" tips " were not to appear in the paper. No
announcement of any kind was made on the
subject. The thing was just done, and has
never been undone. Mr. Taylor died in 1905.
Under the terms of his will Mr. C. P. Scott
became the purchaser of the *Manchester Guardian*
and the governing director of the family company to which it still belongs. Mr. Taylor's
interest in the *Manchester Evening News*, which
had been founded in 1868, passed to his nephew,
Mr. Russell Allen, of Davenham Hall, North-
wich, who became the sole proprietor of that
journal.

The *Guardian* came out of the South African
War in possession of great prestige. For some
eleven years—from about 1903 till 1914—it
had the experience, foreign almost to its genius
and not perhaps altogether to its taste, of being
with the majority, and during these days of a
high party spirit it was the object of a great
personal affection from the Liberal party. Its
name was almost as good for " cheers " in a
Liberal meeting as the name of Gladstone, and
a long and elaborate eulogy of it pronounced
by Mr. Churchill in the Manchester Reform
Club in 1909 evoked from an audience of leading
Liberals an extraordinary demonstration. There
were questions, indeed, on which it continued to
take its own line. Militancy never weakened for
one moment its old and steadfast belief in women's
suffrage. It continued, as it always will continue,

to be genuinely pained and surprised by the widespread popular indifference to proportional representation, or " P.R.," as the standard width of the *Guardian* column has compelled it to christen that seductive cause.

The closing years of this period were darkened by the shadows of war. The *Guardian* steadily discouraged competition in Dreadnoughts which, as the events of the war showed, had nothing to do with naval efficiency. It pleaded for open diplomacy ; suggested a new Triplice of England, France, and Germany ; did and said everything that was possible in the regions of politics, music, art, and travel, to promote Anglo-German friendship. Germany herself would not have it so but, as the calamity came rapidly on in July, 1914, the *Guardian* struggled to the last to avert it. It is curious to turn to the *Guardian* of the last few days before the war and to see the volume of peace sentiment pouring through its pages—Christian and social workers of every kind carrying peace resolutions wherever they were assembled, the Nonconformist churches getting ready to play their historic part. Then Germany broke into Belgium, and the peace movement in England was at an end.

And yet, once in the war, few newspapers contributed more than the *Manchester Guardian* to its strategy. It was almost the first newspaper in England to perceive that the war front was all one, and for at least six months it was advocating alone the " united front " and the "united single command." These ideas were expressed chiefly in the brilliant articles of Mr. Herbert Sidebotham, the "Student of War," who was a principal leader-writer on the paper and had discovered a genius for military criticism during the South African War. It is well known that these articles became extremely authoritative, and did much to make opinion in quarters where to make opinion is to make history. But, for all that, the *Guardian* never ceased to welcome every possible overture of practicable peace. It was the personal friend of President Wilson and the strong supporter of the ideas with which he entered the Peace Conference at Paris.

Since the war the main stem of the paper has put forth two young branches. One of them is the *Manchester Guardian Weekly*, published for the convenience of distant readers and containing week by week the essence of *Guardian* political and literary criticism, and the other the *Manchester Guardian Commercial*, to which has been lent the long practice of the parent paper in business affairs and its high authority with business men.

§ III

As we take our last look at the *Manchester Guardian*, and leave it stepping out on the long stretch of its second century, we see it stamped with an image and superscription. The history of the paper as we look back upon it over one hundred years is an affair of much symmetry,

THE SITE OF THE "MANCHESTER GUARDIAN" BUILDING
AS IT WAS IN 1821

round numbers abounding.* It is exactly one century since it was born ; it is exactly half a century since Charles Prestwich Scott came to Manchester to take up his life's work in its office. Almost his first duty on joining the staff was to take his part in the jubilee celebrations, and there are men still connected with the paper, and others living who have only recently left it, who remember his high post-graduate spirits on that occasion, the joyful noise he made as the omnibuses jolted home out of Cheshire. Mr. Scott's editorship still continues in its full career, and however we weigh and measure what he counts for in its affairs—whether we test it by the number of things both great and small which he decides, by the hours early and late which he gives to its service, or by the number of nights in the week on which it is known in the office that " C. P. is writing the ' long,' " if we even compute it thus by the number of columns he contributes to the paper in the course of a year—he is still not only proprietor and editor of the paper, but its most dominant voice and pen.

His editorship has been one of the illustrious things of journalism at large, but to the *Manchester Guardian* it has been all in all. The history of the *Manchester Guardian* for the last fifty years is the history of his mind. Its sensitiveness to moral ideas, its intolerance of the high hand, its dislike of the magisterial brow are

* Written in 1921.

his. He has given it a new kind of nonconformist conscience which allows for all the arts of life and bases a stern righteousness, not like the old Puritans at the bear-baiting, on hatred of the spectators but rather on love of the victim. His staff know that in the last twenty years his character has not indeed softened, for its tonic and electric quality is still very palpable, but mellowed very greatly beneath the final touches of experience and some private sorrows, and this quality of mellowness is also in the *Guardian*. Its refusal to be terrified by new portents like the sex movement and the Labour movement is merely his spiritual inability to grow old, which shows itself on the physical side in the breathless risks he runs on a bicycle amid the traffic of Manchester when the traffic is at its worst, and at all *Guardian* celebrations, where he dances every dance on the programme except when the next one is, to his visible regret, one of the very modern kind which he has not had the time and opportunity to acquire.

Mr. Scott's life has contained other careers besides that of editorship. He fought several elections as the Liberal candidate for Northeast Manchester, and was eventually elected for the Leigh division of Lancashire in 1895. He took some part in the debates of Parliament, but he was not born, as some men are, to be a private member of the House. He lacked the nerve which the private member needs for the scattering and expense of time, nor had he the

THE SITE TO-DAY.

necessary faculty of holding Roman principles in restful attitudes and beneath ascending wreaths of smoke. In 1905 he left Parliament, made Manchester his centre again, and, though he had never relaxed his hold on the *Guardian*, entered with a definite renewal of the spirit upon his editorship. He came home. It was said of Chamberlain by an observer that he seemed to make fresh beginnings and to discover and develop new powers in the art of public speaking after he was fifty years of age, and the man who made the observation thought the fact an unusual one in human experience. Mr. Scott has bettered the example, and has enlarged the hopes of the sixth and even the seventh decade of human life, for there is no question that his wrist for English prose is easier and more flexible than it was twenty or even ten years ago. The style has reached that high degree of excellence which only comes when style is hid with thought, when it is indeed no longer style but merely the diaphanous vesture of the thing which it is in his mind and of his purpose to say.

Mr. Scott produces the most of his work among the untempered conditions of a newspaper office at night. He is always accessible, and his assistants may without excessive fear and trembling break in upon him with unseasonable topics—with a telegram which has been corrupted in transit and which nobody can emend, with some delicate question perhaps of " giving it " or " leaving it out." The most the tormentor will notice is a brief abstraction, a momentary difficulty in coming to the surface of life. The matter, whatever it be, will receive attention, and if the intruder glances over his shoulder from the door he will see that the mind has picked up the train of its thought again, and that the hand is travelling over the paper beneath the green lamp. He keeps the conscience of the paper and looks closely to its personal form. He cannot away with the word " reliability," will not suffer anything to happen in the " metropolis," and is the only member of his own staff who understands clearly when the conjunction should be " nor " and when it should be " or," and, when one follows the other, what happens next. If any very bad *cliché* appears he will send the proof in which the offence occurs to the responsible subordinate with a pained note of exclamation. It is one of the things that make the difference in the *Guardian* office that the editor requires nothing of his men that he could not do equally well himself.

And if it be asked how all this is done, not only without any dishevelment and discomposure of living, but with rather more than less attention to its airs and graces, the teaching which is contained in the answer is easy to frame and yet hard to follow, since it requires no less than the whole of life. It has been said that the Essays of Emerson were not so much written as assembled out of the notebooks of an unceasing application and, when the greatest of English artists was asked how long it had taken him to make the rough sketch of a human hand, he replied that it had taken him all his life. In the same way the editorship of a great organ, the rapid decision, the finished argument composed against time do not come of a posture towards affairs sometimes assumed and sometimes relaxed. The spring is easy because the poise is always maintained. The burden is carried because it is never laid down. Not even after fifty years of carrying it !